New Trends in Crosslinguistic Influence and Multilingualism Research

SECOND LANGUAGE ACQUISITION
Series Editor: **Professor David Singleton,** *Trinity College, Dublin, Ireland*

This series brings together titles dealing with a variety of aspects of language acquisition and processing in situations where a language or languages other than the native language is involved. Second language is thus interpreted in its broadest possible sense. The volumes included in the series all offer in their different ways, on the one hand, exposition and discussion of empirical findings and, on the other, some degree of theoretical reflection. In this latter connection, no particular theoretical stance is privileged in the series; nor is any relevant perspective – sociolinguistic, psycholinguistic, neurolinguistic, etc. – deemed out of place. The intended readership of the series includes final-year undergraduates working on second language acquisition projects, postgraduate students involved in second language acquisition research, and researchers and teachers in general whose interests include a second language acquisition component.

Full details of all the books in this series and of all our other publications can be found on http://www.multilingual-matters.com, or by writing to Multilingual Matters, St Nicholas House, 31–34 High Street, Bristol BS1 2AW, UK.

SECOND LANGUAGE ACQUISITION
Series Editor: David Singleton, *Trinity College, Dublin, Ireland*

New Trends in Crosslinguistic Influence and Multilingualism Research

Edited by
Gessica De Angelis and Jean-Marc Dewaele

MULTILINGUAL MATTERS
Bristol • Buffalo • Toronto

Library of Congress Cataloging in Publication Data
A catalog record for this book is available from the Library of Congress.
New trends in Crosslinguistic Influence and Multilingualism Research/Edited by
Gessica De Angelis and Jean-Marc Dewaele.
Second Languageb Acquisition: 60
Includes bibliographical references and index.
1. Multilingualism. 2. Language acquisition. I. De Angelis, Gessica- II. Dewaele, Jean-Marc
P115.N46 2011
401'.93–dc23 2011028014

British Library Cataloguing in Publication Data
A catalogue entry for this book is available from the British Library.

ISBN-13: 978-1-84769-442-3 (hbk)
ISBN-13: 978-1-84769-441-6 (pbk)

Multilingual Matters
UK: St Nicholas House, 31–34 High Street, Bristol BS1 2AW, UK.
USA: UTP, 2250 Military Road, Tonawanda, NY 14150, USA.
Canada: UTP, 5201 Dufferin Street, North York, Ontario M3H 5T8, Canada.

Copyright © 2011 Gessica De Angelis, Jean-Marc Dewaele and the authors of individual chapters.

All rights reserved. No part of this work may be reproduced in any form or by any means without permission in writing from the publisher.

The policy of Multilingual Matters/Channel View Publications is to use papers that are natural, renewable and recyclable products, made from wood grown in sustainable forests. In the manufacturing process of our books, and to further support our policy, preference is given to printers that have FSC and PEFC Chain of Custody certification. The FSC and/or PEFC logos will appear on those books where full certification has been granted to the printer concerned.

Typeset by Datapage International Ltd.
Printed and bound in Great Britain by Short Run Press Ltd.

Contents

Introduction
Gessica De Angelis and Jean-Marc Dewaele..................vii

1 Awareness and Affordances: Multilinguals versus
  Bilinguals and their Perceptions of Cognates
  Agnieszka Otwinowska-Kasztelanic..........................1
2 Perceived Redundancy or Crosslinguistic Influence?
  What L3 Learners' Material Can Tell us About the Causes
  of Errors
  Håkan Ringbom...19
3 Crosslinguistic Interaction and Metalinguistic Awareness
  in Third Language Acquisition
  Mariana Bono..25
4 Transfer from L3 German to L2 English in the Domain
  of Tense/Aspect
  Anna S.C. Cheung, Stephen Matthews and Wai Lan Tsang......53
5 Perception of Preposition Errors in Semantically Correct
  versus Erroneous Contexts by Multilingual Advanced
  English as a Foreign Language Learners: Measuring
  Metalinguistic Awareness
  Martha Gibson and Britta Hufeisen.........................74
6 'Luisa and Pedrito's Dog will the Breakfast Eat':
  Interlanguage Transfer and the Role of the Second Language
  Factor
  Laura Sanchez...86
7 Crosslinguistic Influence in Multilingual Language
  Acquisition: Phonology in Third or Additional
  Language Acquisition
  Eva-Maria Wunder...105

Introduction

GESSICA DE ANGELIS and JEAN-MARC DEWAELE

The main purpose of this book is to introduce readers to ongoing work on crosslinguistic influence (CLI) and multilingualism and to highlight the most recent trends in research in this area.

The study of CLI and multilingualism saw a rapid increase in interest over the past 20 years as more and more researchers started considering the combination of different languages as potential sources of CLI on target language production and development. For a long time, the study of CLI was conceived as the study of transfer phenomena from the first language (L1), with little attention being paid to nonnative languages and their possible influence on the CLI process. This gradually changed in the late 1980s and the 1990s, when researchers started to identify evidence of nonnative languages interacting with the L1 and other nonnative languages, sometimes at the same time. Theoretical thinking quickly moved away from the idea that transfer concerned the exchange of information between two languages. As research output increased, it became clear that other languages played a role in the CLI process and that bilingual and multilingual minds could not be assumed to function in exactly the same way. The presence of other languages made a difference, and many studies have focused on finding that difference.

The awareness that multilingualism research has unique characteristics and needs in terms of questions and aims is discussed in several publications (Cenoz & Jessner, 2000; Cenoz et al., 2001, 2003; Hoffman, 2000, 2001a, 2001b; Pavlenko, 2008). Scholars started to ask specific questions about multilingualism rather than bilingualism since some phenomena could not exist without a minimum of three languages in the mind (Bouvy, 2000; Cenoz, 2001; De Angelis, 2005a, 2005b, 2005c, 2007; De Angelis & Selinker, 2001; Edwards & Dewaele, 2007; Falk & Bardel, 2010; Gibson & Hufeisen, 2003; Gibson et al., 2001; Hammarberg, 2001, 2009; Odlin & Jarvis, 2004; Ringbom, 2007). In addition to evidence of CLI from nonnative languages, an overall positive effect of bi/multilingualism on third or additional language learning was found, particularly in additive learning contexts (Brohy, 2001; Cenoz, 2003; Cenoz & Hoffmann, 2003; Jessner, 2008; Keshavarz & Astaneh, 2004; Sagasta Errasti, 2003; Sanz, 2000).

So far, evidence of CLI in multilinguals has been identified in most fields, including phonology (Gut, 2010; Kim, 2009), morphology (Clyne & Cassia, 1999; Lowie, 2000), syntax (Flynn et al., 2004; Klein, 1995; Leung, 2009; Rothman & Cabrelli Amaro, 2010) and pragmatics (Safont Jordà, 2005a, 2005b; Serratrice et al., 2004).

Perhaps one of the most investigated areas to date has been that of language distance and typology since it became clear to researchers that language distance alone was not sufficient to explain some CLI phenomena observed in multilingual production. Several scholars examined the topic with different language combinations (Clyne, 1997; Clyne & Cassia, 1999; Dewaele, 1998; Odlin & Jarvis, 2004; Selinker & Baumgartner-Cohen, 1995), including non-Western languages (Foroodi-Nejad & Paradis, 2009; Hacohen & Schaeffer, 2007; Kim, 2009). Specific instances of CLI or the overall effect of prior language knowledge on a target language were attributed to the presence or absence of literacy in the nonnative languages, L2 status and/or a heightened awareness of languages (Charkova, 2004; De Angelis & Selinker, 2001; Galambos & Goldin-Meadow, 1990; Jessner, 1999, 2006; Kemp, 2001; Lasagabaster, 2001; Swain et al., 1990; Thomas, 1992; Williams & Hammarberg, 1998). The study of CLI has changed radically since it is no longer conceived as a one-language-to-another kind of phenomenon but as a process that concerns all language knowledge in the mind, including the influence of the nonnative languages on the L1 (Jarvis & Pavlenko, 2008; Pavlenko & Jarvis, 2002). Findings suggest that language interactions affect the learning process as well as the cognitive development of individuals.

There are ongoing debates in the field of CLI on aspects of the multilingual language production process and evidence from this line of research has been increasingly used to explain how and when native and nonnative knowledge is used in language production. Grosjean (1998, 2001) has created an influential psycholinguistic framework to explain the interaction between languages. His language-mode hypothesis is based on the fact that the bilingual's languages are active to varying degrees when an interaction takes place. There is usually a base, fully active, language, and there are other language(s) that can be active to varying degrees. Grosjean defines language mode as 'the state of activation of the bilingual's languages and language processing mechanisms at a certain point in time' (2001: 3).

The bilingual can be in a complete monolingual mode at one end of the continuum when 'they are interacting only with (or listening to) monolinguals of one – or the other – of the languages they know. One language is active and the other is deactivated' (Grosjean, 1998: 136). The same person can be in a bilingual language mode at the other end of the continuum, when they are communicating with (or listening to) bilinguals who share their two (or more) languages and where language mixing may take place (i.e. code-switching and borrowing). In this case, both languages are active but the one that is used as the main language of processing (the base of the matrix language) is more active than the other. These are end points, and bilinguals also find themselves at intermediary points depending on the factors mentioned above. (Grosjean, 1998: 136)

The bilingual has to decide at any given point in time, usually quite unconsciously, which language to use and how much of the other language is needed (Grosjean, 2001: 2). Sometimes, however, some influence of the deactivated language is detected in the base language, which is the most highly activated language. Grosjean (2008: 77) points out that 'future research will have to investigate the underlying mechanism (...) that make the stronger language "seep through" despite the fact that it has been deactivated (...)'.

Other researchers have focused on how the multilingual lexicon is organized (Abunuwara, 1992; Cenoz *et al.*, 2003; Pavlenko, 2009) and how multilingual memory functions (De Groot & Hoeks, 1995), leading to stimulating discussions on the speech production process (De Bot, 1992; Dewaele, 1998; Grosjean, 2001, 2008; Hammarberg, 2009). In addition to these, numerous studies focused on the lexicon, word selection problems and tip-of-the-tongue states, where questions on the use of prior knowledge in comprehension and production processes remained central (Cenoz *et al.*, 2003; Dewaele, 2001; Dijkstra & van Hell, 2003; Ecke, 2001; Ecke & Hall, 2000; Festman, 2009; Jessner, 2003; Ringbom, 2007; Schönpflug, 2000, 2003; Singleton, 2003; Van Hell & Dijkstra, 2002; Wei, 2003).

Recent research has also looked into the possible causes of CLI among bilinguals. Festman (to appear) has demonstrated that some bilinguals are more susceptible to CLI than others despite similar levels of language proficiency and language mode. She argues that the increased CLI is linked to language control and related to executive functions, in particular to inhibition.

There is a general awareness that CLI is a broader and more complex process than the one-to-one type of phenomenon researchers had initially focused on. Most academic discussions now take into account the presence of nonnative languages and attempt to account for such knowledge. The collection of contributions in the present volume will give the reader a general idea of where CLI research is heading now in the areas of syntax, lexis and phonology. The authors, both veteran researchers and newcomers to the field, situate their research in current debates in terms of theory and empirical data. In the present volume, readers will find several chapters discussing issues of lexis, metalinguistic awareness and L2 status. The data have been collected from participants with a wide combination of languages: besides English, German, French and Spanish, there is Finnish, Swedish, Polish, Chinese and Catalan.

Agnieszka Otwinowska-Kasztelanic argues for the existence of a relationship between the theory of affordances and crosslinguistic similarities in the area of lexis, with special emphasis on the role of cognate vocabulary in the learning process. Reference to Gibson's theory of affordances has appeared recently in trilingualism research (see Dewaele, 2010; Singleton & Aronin, 2007). Her research suggests that multilinguals are advantaged over bilinguals in noticing the role of lexical similarities and have a wider range of affordances available to them during learning that bilinguals do not have at their disposal.

Ringbom's contribution also focuses on the learning process, this time in relation to learners' use of redundancies. He revisits the notion of redundancy that George (1972) proposed several years ago and suggests it should be brought into current debates on CLI and multilingualism. He argues that learners tend to conserve effort as a strategy to simplify the learning task. Whenever a target language category does not exist in the L1 or a native language, the learner perceives it as redundant. As a result, this category is omitted at the early stages of learning.

Bono's chapter focuses on multilingual competence (mainly French, Spanish, English and German, with a few participants having Vietnamese, Hebrew, Wolof and Arabic as L1s) and the role of crosslinguistic interactions and metalinguistic awareness in the production of lexis. She argues in favor of the L2 status overriding typological proximity in production. She also claims that the study of language switches should include the study of metalinguistic sequences and argues that learners carry out conscious crosslinguistic comparisons based on L2 data.

Interesting evidence of reverse transfer from German L3 to English L2 can be found in Cheung, Matthews and Tsang's chapter who worked with Chinese (Cantonese) L1 students. Drawing on the distinction between the use of the past tense with or without current relevance in Chinese, English and German, they hypothesize that learners with knowledge of German are more likely to use the English present perfect tense when referring to past events without current relevance. Their results confirm the hypothesis: Those who have studied German as a third language are more likely to produce and accept the use of the present perfect without current relevance in English.

Gibson and Hufeisen also present a study involving German and English. They focus on EFL learners' perception of spatial prepositions and how these are used in production. The authors asked learners to complete a grammaticality judgment task of prepositional errors involving *of*, *in*, *at* and *on* and found differences based on learning experience.

Experienced language learners seem more accurate in their judgments, which is explained in terms of these learners having enhanced multilingual abilities.

Laura Sanchez presents a study on the L2 status and its role in CLI. Since the L2 status is often difficult to tease apart from typological distance, the author designed a study where the two are kept separate. She tested two hypotheses with Spanish and Catalan L1 speakers learning German and English. Her findings suggest that in third-language acquisition, nonnative languages are more likely to be activated than the mother tongue regardless of typology.

The last chapter by Eva-Maria Wunder contributes to the current debate on CLI and phonology, an area where only a few studies are currently available. The author examines the aspiration patterns of voiceless stops with L3 learners of Spanish with German L1 and English L2. She recorded learners performing a read-on-your-own task and analyzed the degree of aspiration of the voiceless stops in stressed onset position (VOT measurements). Her results identify the existence of nonnative language influence as well as forms of combined CLI with an underlying L1 effect.

Acknowledgments

A word of thanks, finally, to the many friends and colleagues who acted as reviewers for the contributions in the present volume: Patricia Bayona, Raphael Berthele, Jasone Cenoz, Bjorn Hammarberg, Britta Hufeisen, Scott Jarvis, Ulrike Jessner, Nicole Marx, Håkan Ringbom, Laura Sanchez, David Singleton and John Witney.

References

Abunuwara, E. (1992) The structure of the trilingual lexicon. *European Journal of Cognitive Psychology* 4 (4), 311–322.

Bouvy, C. (2000) Towards the construction of a theory of cross-linguistic transfer. In J. Cenoz and U. Jessner (eds) *English in Europe: The Acquisition of a Third Language* (pp. 143–156). Clevedon: Multilingual Matters.

Brohy, C. (2001) Generic and/or specific advantages of bilingualism in a dynamic plurilingual situation: The case of French as official L3 in the school of Samedan (Switzerland). *International Journal of Bilingual Education and Bilingualism* 4 (1), 38–49.

Cenoz, J. (2001) The effect of linguistic distance, L2 status and age on cross-linguistic influence in third language acquisition. In J. Cenoz, B. Hufeisen and U. Jessner (eds) *Cross-linguistic Influence in Third Language Acquisition: Psycholinguistic Perspectives* (pp. 8–20). Clevedon: Multilingual Matters.

Cenoz, J. (2003) The additive effect of bilingualism in third language acquisition: A review. *International Journal of Bilingualism* 7 (1), 71–87.

Cenoz, J. and Hoffmann, C. (2003) Acquiring a third language: What role does bilingualism play? *International Journal of Bilingualism* 7 (1), 1–6.

Cenoz, J. and Jessner, U. (eds) (2000) *English in Europe: The Acquisition of a Third Language*. Clevedon: Multilingual Matters.

Cenoz, J., Hufeisen, B. and Jessner, U. (eds) (2001) *Cross-linguistic Influence in Third Language Acquisition: Psycholinguistic Perspectives*. Clevedon: Multilingual Matters.

Cenoz, J., Hufeisen, B. and Jessner, U. (eds) (2003) *The Multilingual Lexicon*. Dordrecht: Kluwer Academic.

Charkova, K.D. (2004) Early foreign language education and metalinguistic development: A study of monolingual, bilingual and trilingual children on noun definition tasks. *Annual Review of Language Acquisition* 3 (1), 51–88.

Clyne, M. (1997) Some of the things trilinguals do. *The International Journal of Bilingualism* 1 (2), 95–116.

Clyne, M. and Cassia, P. (1999) Trilingualism, immigration and relatedness of languages. *ITL Review of Applied Linguistics* 123–124, 57–74.

De Angelis, G. (2005a) Interlanguage transfer of function words. *Language Learning* 55 (3), 379–414.

De Angelis, G. (2005b) Multilingualism and non-native lexical transfer: An identification problem. *International Journal of Multilingualism* 2 (1), 1–25.

De Angelis, G. (2005c) The acquisition of languages beyond the L2: Psycholinguistic perspectives. *Rassegna Italiana di Linguistica Applicata* 2–3, 397–409.

De Angelis, G. (2007) *Third or Additional Language Acquisition*. Clevedon: Multilingual Matters.

De Angelis, G. and Selinker, L. (2001) Interlanguage transfer and competing linguistic systems in the multilingual mind. In J. Cenoz, B. Hufeisen and U. Jessner (eds) *Cross-linguistic Influence in Third Language Acquisition: Psycholinguistic Perspectives* (pp. 42–58). Clevedon: Multilingual Matters.

De Bot, K. (1992) A bilingual production model: Levelt's 'speaking' model adapted. *Applied Linguistics* 13, 1, 1–24.

De Groot, A. and Hoeks, J. (1995) The development of bilingual memory: Evidence from word translation by trilinguals. *Language Learning* 45 (4), 683–724.

Dewaele, J-M. (1998) Lexical inventions: French interlanguage as L2 versus L3. *Applied Linguistics* 19 (4), 471–490.

Dewaele, J-M. (2001) Activation or inhibition? The interaction of L1, L2 and L3 on the language mode continuum. In J. Cenoz, B. Hufeisen and U. Jessner (eds) *Cross-linguistic Influence in Third Language Acquisition: Psycholinguistic Perspectives* (pp. 69–89). Clevedon: Multilingual Matters.

Dewaele, J-M. (2010) Multilingualism and affordances: Variation in self-perceived communicative competence and communicative anxiety in French L1, L2, L3 and L4. *International Review of Applied Linguistics* 48, 105–129.

Dijkstra, T. and van Hell, J.V. (2003) Testing the language mode hypothesis using trilinguals. *International Journal of Bilingual Education and Bilingualism* 6, 2–16.

Ecke, P. (2001) Lexical retrieval in a third language: Evidence from errors and tip-of-the-tongue states. In J. Cenoz, B. Hufeisen and U. Jessner (eds) *Cross-linguistic Influence in Third Language Acquisition: Psycholinguistic Perspectives* (pp. 90–114). Clevedon: Multilingual Matters.

Ecke, P. and Hall, C.J. (2000) Lexikalischer fehler in Deutsch als drittsprache: Translexikalischer einfluss auf 3 ebenen der mentalen repräsentation. [Lexical errors in German as a third language. Translexical influence in three levels of the mental representation.] *Deutsch als Fremdsprache* [German as a foreign language] 1, 31–37.

Edwards, M. and Dewaele, J-M. (2007) Trilingual conversations: A window into multicompetence? *The International Journal of Bilingualism* 11, 221–241.

Falk, Y. and Bardel, C. (2010) The study of the role of the background languages in third language acquisition. The state of the art. *International Review of Applied Linguistics* 48, 87–90.

Festman, J. (2009) *Three Languages in Mind. How Activation, Inhibition and Control Underlie Trilingual Lexical Production.* Saarbrücken: VDM.

Festman, J. (to appear) Language control of late bilinguals. *Bilingualism: Language and Cognition.*

Flynn, S., Foley, C. and Vinnitskaya, I. (2004) The cumulative-enhancement model of language acquisition: Comparing adults' and children's patters of development in first, second and third language acquisition of relative clauses. *International Journal of Multilingualism* 1 (1), 3–16.

Foroodi-Nejad, F. and Paradis, J. (2009) Crosslinguistic transfer in the acquisition of compound words in Persian-English bilinguals. *Bilingualism: Language and Cognition*, 12 (4), 411–427.

Galambos, J.S. and Goldin-Meadow, S. (1990) The effects of learning two languages on levels of metalinguistic awareness. *Cognition* 34, 1–56.

George, H.V. (1972) *Common Errors in Language Learning.* Rowley, MA: Newbury House.

Gibson, M. and Hufeisen, B. (2003) Investigating the role of prior foreign language knowledge: Translating from an unknown language into a known foreign language. In J. Cenoz, B. Hufeisen and U. Jessner (eds) *The Multilingual Lexicon* (pp. 87–102). Dordrecht: Kluwer Academic.

Gibson, M., Hufeisen, B. and Libben, G. (2001) Learners of German as an L3 and their production of German prepositional verbs. In J. Cenoz, B. Hufeisen and U. Jessner (eds) *Cross-linguistic Influence in Third Language Acquisition: Psycholinguistic Perspectives* (pp. 138–148). Clevedon: Multilingual Matters.

Grosjean, F. (1998) Studying bilinguals: Methodological and conceptual issues. *Bilingualism: Language and Cognition* 1 (2), 131–149.

Grosjean, F. (2001) The bilingual's language modes. In J. Nicol (ed.) *One Mind, Two Languages: Bilingual Language Processing* (pp. 1–22). Oxford: Blackwell.

Grosjean, F. (2008) *Studying Bilinguals.* Oxford: Oxford University Press.

Gut, U. (2010) Cross-linguistic influence in L3 phonological acquisition. *International Journal of Multilingualism* 7, 19–38.

Hacohen, A. and Schaeffer, J. (2007) Subject realization in early Hebrew/English bilingual acquisition: The role of crosslinguistic influence. *Bilingualism: Language and Cognition* 10 (3), 333–344.

Hammarberg, B. (2001) Roles of L1 and L2 in L3 production and acquisition. In J. Cenoz, B. Hufeisen and U. Jessner (eds) *Cross-linguistic Influence in Third Language Acquisition: Psycholinguistic Perspectives* (pp. 21–41). Clevedon: Multilingual Matters.

Hammarberg, B. (ed.) (2009) *Processes in Third Language Acquisition.* Edinburgh: Edinburgh University Press.

Hoffman, C. (2000) Bilingual and trilingual competence: Problems of description and differentiation. *Estudios de Sociolingüística* 1, 83–92.

Hoffman, C. (2001a) Towards a description of trilingual competence. *International Journal of Bilingualism* 5, 1–17.

Hoffman, C. (2001b) The status of trilingualism in bilingualism studies. In J. Cenoz, U. Jessner and B. Hufeisen (eds) *Looking Beyond Second Language Acquisition: Studies in Tri- and Multilingualism* (pp. 13–25). Tübingen: Stauffenburg Verlag.

Jarvis, S. and Pavlenko, A. (2008) *Crosslinguistic Influence in Language and Cognition.* Abingdon: Routledge.

Jessner, U. (1999) Metalinguistic awareness in multilinguals: Cognitive aspects of third language learning. *Language Awareness* 8 (3–4), 201–209.
Jessner, U. (2003) The nature of cross-linguistic interaction in the multilingual system. In J. Cenoz, B. Hufeisen and U. Jessner (eds) *The Multilingual Lexicon* (pp. 45–55). Dordrecht: Kluwer Academic.
Jessner, U. (2006) *Linguistic Awareness in Multilinguals. English as a Third Language*. Edinburgh: Edinburgh University Press.
Jessner, U. (2008) Teaching third languages: Findings, trends and challenges. *Language Teaching* 41 (1), 15–56.
Kemp, C. (2001) Metalinguistic awareness in multilinguals: Implicit and explicit grammatical awareness and its relationship with language experience and language attainment. Unpublished PhD thesis, University of Edinburgh.
Keshavarz, M.H. and Astaneh, H. (2004) The impact of bilinguality on the learning of English vocabulary as a foreign language (L3). *Bilingual Education and Bilingualism* 7 (4), 295–303.
Kim, Y. (2009) Crosslinguistic influence on phonological awareness for Korean-English bilingual children. *Reading and Writing: An Interdisciplinary Journal*, 22 (7), 843–861.
Klein, E.C. (1995) Second versus third language acquisition: Is there a difference? *Language Learning* 45 (3), 419–465.
Lasagabaster, D. (2001) The effect of knowledge about the L1 on foreign language skills and grammar. *International Journal of Bilingual Education and Bilingualism* 4 (5), 310–331.
Leung, Y-K.I. (ed.) (2009) *Third Language Acquisition and Universal Grammar*. Bristol: Multilingual Matters.
Lowie, W. (2000) Cross-linguistic influence on morphology in the bilingual mental lexicon. *Studia Linguistica* 52 (4), 175–185.
Odlin, T. and Jarvis, S. (2004) Same source, different outcomes: A study of Swedish influence on the acquisition of English in Finland. *International Journal of Multilingualism* 1 (2), 123–140.
Pavlenko, A. (2008) Bi- and multilingualism as a metaphor for research. *Bilingualism: Language and Cognition* 11 (2), 197–201.
Pavlenko, A. (2009) (ed.) *The Bilingual Mental Lexicon: Interdisciplinary Approaches*. Bristol: Multilingual Matters.
Pavlenko, A. and Jarvis, S. (2002) Bidirectional transfer. *Applied Linguistics* 23 (2), 190–214.
Ringbom, H. (2007) *Crosslinguistic Similarity in Foreign Language Learning*. Clevedon: Multilingual Matters.
Rothman, J. and Cabrelli Amaro, J. (2010) What variables condition syntactic transfer? A look at the L3 initial state. *Second Language Research* 26 (2), 189–218.
Safont Jordà, M.P. (2005a) Pragmatic production of third language learners of English: A focus on request acts modifiers. *International Journal of Multilingualism* 2 (2), 84–104.
Safont Jordà, M.P. (2005b) *Third Language Learners. Pragmatic Production and Awareness*. Clevedon: Multilingual Matters.
Sagasta Errasti, M.P. (2003) Acquiring writing skills in a third language: The positive effects of bilingualism. *International Journal of Bilingualism* 7 (1), 27–42.
Sanz, C. (2000) Bilingual education enhances third language acquisition: Evidence from Catalonia. *Applied Psycholinguistics* 21, 23–44.
Schönpflug, U. (2000) Word fragment completions in the second and third language. In J. Cenoz and U. Jessner (eds) *English in Europe. The Acquisition of a Third Language* (pp. 121–142). Clevedon, Avon, UK: Multilingual Matters.

Schönpflug, U. (2003) The transfer-appropriate-processing approach and the trilingual's organization of the lexicon. In J. Cenoz, B. Hufeisen and U. Jessner (eds) *The Multilingual Lexicon* (pp. 27–43). Dordrecht: Kluwer Academic.

Selinker, L. and Baumgartner-Cohen, B. (1995) Multiple language acquisition: 'Damn it, why can't I keep these two languages apart?' *Language, Culture and Curriculum* 8 (2), 115–121.

Serratrice, L., Sorace, A. and Paoli, S. (2004) Crosslinguistic influence at the syntax-pragmatics interface: Subjects and objects in English-Italian bilingual and monolingual acquisition. *Bilingualism: Language and Cognition* 7 (3), 183–205.

Singleton, D. (2003) Perspectives on the multilingual lexicon: A critical synthesis. In J. Cenoz, B. Hufeisen and U. Jessner (eds) *The Multilingual Lexicon* (pp. 167–176). Dordrecht: Kluwer Academic.

Singleton, D. and Aronin, L. (2007) Multiple language learning in the light of the theory of affordances. *Innovation in Language Learning and Teaching* 1, 83–96.

Swain, M., Lapkin, S., Rowen, N. and Hart, D. (1990) The role of mother tongue literacy in third language learning. *Language, Culture and Curriculum* 3 (1), 65–81.

Thomas, J. (1992) Metalinguistic awareness in second- and third-language learning. In R.J. Harris (ed.) *Cognitive Processing in Bilinguals* (pp. 531–545). Amsterdam: North-Holland.

Van Hell, J.G. and Dijkstra, T. (2002) Foreign language knowledge can influence native language performance in exclusively native contexts. *Psychonomic Bulletin and Review* 9 (4), 780–789.

Wei, L. (2003) Activation of lemmas in the multilingual mental lexicon and transfer in third language learning. In J. Cenoz, B. Hufeisen and U. Jessner (eds) *The Multilingual Lexicon* (pp. 57–70.) Dordrecht: Kluwer Academic.

Williams, S. and Hammarberg, B. (1998) Language switches in L3 production: Implications for a polyglot speaking model. *Applied Linguistics* 19 (3), 295–333.

Chapter 1
Awareness and Affordances: Multilinguals versus Bilinguals and their Perceptions of Cognates

AGNIESZKA OTWINOWSKA-KASZTELANIC

Introduction

The theory of affordances has recently been discussed with reference to domains as diverse as ecological psychology, industrial design, human–computer interaction and, finally, language acquisition, where it sheds new light on the meaning and importance of awareness phenomena. The present chapter briefly discusses the theory of affordances and its relation to language acquisition, attempting to show the link between affordances available to language learners and their awareness of crosslinguistic lexical similarities. The chapter points to the fact that although the presence of cognate vocabulary in L1, L2 and L*n* may constitute a set of affordances, these affordances are not easily available to all language learners, and that multilinguals and bilinguals differ in their awareness of the role of crosslinguistic similarities. The research presented investigates the differences in the range of lexical affordances available to Polish multilingual and bilingual learners of English. Finally, the chapter presents some implications for teacher training and syllabus design based on the research findings.

The Theory of Affordances and Second Language Acquisition

The theory of affordances was first proposed by perceptual psychologist James J. Gibson (1977, 1979). It dealt with the mutual relationships between the organism and its environment in the area of perception. For conventional theories, perception is a one-way process where an organism processes the image formed by the stimuli in the environment. According to Gibson, however, perception of the environment is also the perception of the self: the environment and the organism are mutually complementary. The organism perceives its environment as a set of possibilities that the environment provides or affords. According to Gibson (1977: 67), an affordance is 'a specific combination of the properties of [the environment's] substance and its surfaces taken with reference to the animal'. In other words, affordances are the perceived opportunities for action provided for the observer by an environment. Hence, they can be understood as the possibilities that an object or environment offers (or appears to offer) to the organism for action or functioning, or chances for the organism to fulfil its goals. Norman (1988, 1999), who popularized the theory within the field of interaction design, developed the term of 'perceived affordance'. This distinction makes the concept dependent not only on the physical capabilities of the actor but also on the actor's goals, plans, values, beliefs and experience. As he puts it: '... the term affordance refers to the perceived and actual properties of the thing, primarily those fundamental properties that determine just how the thing could possibly be used' (1999: 9). Effectively, Norman's affordance 'suggests' how an object can be used and interacted with.

As for connections between perceptual psychology and linguistics, Gibson's ecological psychology affected the development of a linguistic theory of situations (Barwise & Perry, 1983). The theory, together with Norman's idea of perceived affordances has been used to point out that language, like any other environment, offers certain affordances to its users. MacWhinney (1999) noted that language plays an important role in communicating information about situational affordances. Drawing on his observations, Segalowitz (1997, 2001) suggested that taking advantage of affordances that language offers plays a role in individual differences in second language acquisition. According to him, learners may vary with regard to the flexibility and fluency required to deal with language. However, their L2 performance may also involve sensitivity to environmental affordances, that is, the ability to adjust to the changing linguistic and non-linguistic context. Segalowitz (2001) claimed that affordances are important for learning, on condition that the learner is aware of them, whereas van Lier (2000: 252) emphasized the fact that an affordance affords further action but does not cause or trigger it. According to Segalowitz (2001: 15), although a given language, like any physical environment, possesses affordances and supports a particular set of constructions, the constructions are 'available for packaging a message if the speaker knows how to use them. These constructions afford the possibility of making certain messages but not others, and make some messages easier to communicate than others'. As Tella and Harjanne put it:

> Affordances speak a language of their own. Some actors can understand that language better than others. Others can be completely deaf to that language. [...] Linguistic affordances are for us to take advantage of, but they do not spontaneously engage us, unless we are active enough to notice them and proactive enough to start exploiting them. (Tella & Harjanne, 2007: 502)

In other words, language learners have at their disposal potential affordances connected with their language resources and their language-learning environments. Thus, learning or acquiring a language involves 'attuning one's attention system to perceive the communicative affordances provided by the linguistic environment' (Segalowitz, 2001: 15–16). Segalowitz's framework, where learning is seen as a complex interaction between individuals and the context in which they find themselves, ties up with Schmidt's noticing hypothesis (1990, 1998, 2001), which states that every aspect of second language acquisition involves attention. 'Noticing' can be described as a necessary condition for the input to become intake in language learning, although there is no agreement as to what part of the noticed input can be assimilated. According to Schmidt (1990), input equals intake, provided it is perceived as a personal reference (a subjective experience) and explicitly reflected upon. For Gass (1997), some elements of input do not automatically become intake, whereas Gass et al. (2003) see attention as a complex phenomenon related to noticing in language processing. Taking the discussion a step further, one can assume that without noticing certain available affordances, the learner may not be able to use them. Thus, affordances are connected with the perception of certain opportunities, and as a result, for affordances to be perceived, the learner must be sensitive to the relevant information and attend to that information. Thus, affordances associated with language learning and use will be available only to those learners who are aware of them. According to Singleton and Aronin (2007: 85), 'the higher the level of language awareness is, the more effectively language-related possibilities are likely to be perceived and capitalised upon'.

Affordances and Crosslinguistic Lexical Similarities

Human beings, like other organisms, assess environmental stimuli to decide if they will enhance or hinder the fulfilling of their needs and goals. Similarly, language users and learners should intuitively judge whether phenomena within language and across languages may be utilized to enhance communication, as pointed out by Schumann (1997) in his discussion of stimulus appraisal. According to Odlin (2006: 30), '[w]ith specific reference to interlingual identifications, we can surmise that stimulus appraisal entails, *inter alia*, a judgement about communicative utility'. Crosslinguistic similarities can definitely be placed among the phenomena enhancing both communication and language learning (Odlin, 1989, 2003; Ringbom, 1987, 2007). Wode (1983, cited in Odlin 2006) suggested that learners need to notice 'a crucial similarity' between the native and the target language, whereas Odlin (1989: 77) stated that 'similarities and dissimilarities in word forms, along with similarities and dissimilarities in word meanings, play a major role in how quickly a particular foreign language may be learned by speakers of another language'. What follows is that the existence of cognate words in the learner's L1, L2 and Ln may enhance the process of language learning when the learner is able to judge their communicative utility.

Cognates are commonly defined as 'words in different languages, which have descended from a common parent word' (Schmitt, 1997: 209). However, as claimed by Otwinowska-Kasztelanic (2001) and Rusiecki (2002), the group of cognates also comprises words borrowed from one language to another (e.g. computer and hamburger) or borrowed independently by some languages (e.g. sputnik and robot). Thus, cognates should be understood as words that have descended from a common parent word, have been borrowed from Lx to Ly or have been borrowed independently by the two languages. Defined in such a way, cognates exist in European languages both close and distant typologically (e.g. English: *optimistic, computer, zebra*; Polish: *optymistyczny, komputer, zebra*; German: *optimistisch, Computer, Zebra*). For instance, for Polish and English, the number of cognates exceeds 2500 items, as noted by Otwinowska-Kasztelanic (2007, 2009). It is not difficult to notice that Latin- and Greek-based words are also quite common in formal styles and registers used by educated European speakers in their L1. As for English, Nation and Meara (2002: 49) point out that 'almost all the basic Anglo-Saxon words have parallel forms based on Latin and Greek, which are used in particular, specialist discourse'. This, in turn, entails that English – the European *lingua franca* – can serve as a mediation tool between the native language and other European languages.

The awareness of cognates may enhance language learning, which was proved experimentally (Haastrup, 1991; Jessner, 1999; Otwinowska-Kasztelanic, 2009, 2010; Ringbom, 2007; Swan, 1997). Ringbom (2007: 104) states that crosslinguistic similarity is 'an important variable in the use of learning strategies: how the learner tries to enhance the effectiveness of learning'. However, according to Swan (1997: 161), lexical similarity does not always lead to the enhanced mastery of L2 vocabulary, whereas Schmitt (1997: 209) states that cognates may be 'an excellent resource for both guessing the meaning and remembering new words. Of course, learners do not automatically accept cognates as equivalent'. On the other hand, Odlin (2002: 260, original emphasis) points to the fact that '[t]he actual similarity or dissimilarity of forms and meanings is only one factor at work in transfer; the *judgement* of each individual learner matters as much'. On the basis of the previous discussion of affordances and the noticing phenomena, one can assume that cognates can enhance language learning only if noticed, recognized and accepted by the learner. Thus, cognate word forms, even if they do not constitute 'crucial similarity' between the native and the target language, may be regarded as a set of affordances in learning a foreign language since their communicative utility cannot be underestimated. Proactive learners will be aware of crosslinguistic similarities and will make use of those affordances.

Affordances in Noticing Crosslinguistic Similarities: Bilingualism and Multilingualism

The learner's ability to notice that L1 offers certain affordances in L2 learning depends on several factors. According to Kellerman (1977, 1983), one of the key issues in the understanding of why certain learners fail to acknowledge the relationship between the mother tongue and the language learned is the typological and the psychotypological distance between L1 and L2. Crosslinguistic influence is stronger between languages that are typologically close (Duškova, 1984), such as Polish and Slovak. In the case of vocabulary in European languages, positive transfer (noticing and using cognates) as well as negative transfer (overusing false friends) will be strongest within each of the major typological groups: Germanic, Slavonic or Romance. However, the situation is different across typological boundaries. For instance, Otwinowska-Kasztelanic (2010) has pointed out that overusing false friends by Polish advanced learners speaking English is rare and may be considered a feature of the learner's idiolect.

Crosslinguistic influence also decreases when languages are perceived as distant by the learner (Kellerman, 1983; Ringbom, 1986; Singleton, 2006). Ringbom (2006: 38) discusses perceived and assumed similarity, as opposed to objective similarity of language items and forms. If the learner perceives an L2 to be significantly different or distant from his or her L1, he or she may not be aware or may not even notice certain formal similarities between the two. Thus, awareness and readiness to use the affordances offered by the cognate vocabulary depends, first of all, on the perceived psychotypological distance between L1 and L2.

Another important reason why noticing crosslinguistic similarities differs from learner to learner is the differences in the level of the learner's language knowledge and the number of languages known. There are numerous accounts of how monolinguals differ from bilinguals and how the latter differ from multilinguals in terms of general language awareness, facilitated language learning, language learning strategies or metalinguistic awareness (Cenoz & Genesse, 1998; Cenoz *et al.*, 2001; Herdina & Jessner, 2002; Hoffmann, 2001; Jessner, 1999, 2008). According to post-structural definitions (e.g. Macnamara, 1967), even beginning L2 learners may be called bilingual; however, their knowledge and awareness are incomparable with those of advanced learners. Since bilingualism is understood as possessing at least minimal competence in one of the four skills of L2, and multilingualism means a constant interplay between languages, the environment and cognitive processes, multilinguals are advantaged over bilinguals in learning languages. Multilinguals have more 'experience' in language learning and using and have more chances of interacting with the environment. Their multilingualism also facilitates their metalinguistic knowledge and awareness. That is why it is possible to assume that they will have more linguistic affordances at their disposal. As Singleton and Aronin (2007: 85) put it, '[i]t is obvious that more potential affordances are at the disposal of multilinguals than of other language users. Self-evidently, multilinguals have larger overall linguistic repertoires than other language users'. Having acknowledged that lexical crosslinguistic similarities may constitute a set of affordances in learning a language, it is possible to say that multilinguals should be advantaged over bilinguals in noticing such affordances.

Investigating Awareness of English–Polish Cognate Vocabulary: The Aim and Design of the Research

The aim of the present research on Polish students of English was to estimate the range of affordances available to them through their awareness of cognate vocabulary. For the purpose of the research, cognate vocabulary was defined as words in English and Polish that have descended from a common parent word, were borrowed from English into Polish or were borrowed independently by the two languages. It was assumed that the affordances available to the learners depend on their perception of the psychotypological distance between English and Polish, their level of English and the number of languages they know. It was hypothesized that there is a positive relationship between the level of English and the awareness of cognates. It was also hypothesized that there is a positive relationship between multilingualism and the awareness of cognates. In the present study, the awareness of cognates was defined as the knowledge of which English and Polish words are cognates and how many such words there are.

The research, which surveyed 512 respondents, took place in Warsaw, Poland, in the years 2006–2008 and involved responding to a Polish-language version of a questionnaire (see Appendix) within the time limit of 10 minutes. While completing the questionnaire, the respondents were not allowed to consult each other. The wording of the questionnaire items left no doubt about what cognates were since the respondents were asked to enumerate and assess the number of 'words whose form and meaning are similar in English and Polish'. The same questionnaire had been previously used in the experimental studies on advanced Polish learners of English and its reliability had been supported by results of tasks concerning recognition and production of cognates (Otwinowska-Kasztelanic, 2009, 2010).

The respondents to the questionnaire were three groups of bilingual Polish learners of English, as well as a group of multilingual students proficient in at least three European languages. The group from now on called Elementary included 95 beginning learners (level A1/A2 of the Common European Framework) from a renowned private language school in Warsaw, aged between 19 and 35. The group from now on called Intermediate consisted of 134 intermediate level (B1/B2) students from Warsaw University and a college of information technology, aged between 19 and 24. The group from now on called Advanced comprised 200 students of the Institute of English Studies, Warsaw University (level C1/C2), aged between 19 and 22. The last group, from now on called Multilinguals, included 83 students of the Institute of English Studies, aged between 19 and 25, who were at least trilingual. Their native language was Polish; they were all advanced learners of English as L2 (C1/C2) and advanced learners of L3 languages (C1 or C2 in Spanish, French, Portuguese, Italian, Russian or German). In addition, most Multilinguals learned various L4 or L5 languages (A1 to B2 in Spanish, Portuguese, Catalan, German, French or Italian). None of them indicated knowing Latin or Greek.

For the purpose of the current study, only Questions 1, 5, 6 and 7 of the questionnaire were taken into account. Question 1 focused on the perceptions of the typological distance between English and Polish, and Questions 6 and 7 focused on the respondents' beliefs concerning the number of cognates known to them that were present between the two languages. In Question 5, the respondents were asked to enumerate five English–Polish cognates. Questions 5, 6 and 7 measured the respondents' awareness of cognate vocabulary. In accordance with the theoretical considerations discussed in the previous sections, it was assumed that the awareness of crosslinguistic lexical similarities, and hence, the range of affordances available to the learners, depends on three basic independent variables. These are the learners' perception of the psychotypological distance between English and Polish, their level of English and the fact that they are bilingual or multilingual. For the purpose of the study, the respondents' level of English was graded in the following way: Elementary, 1 point; Intermediate, 2 points; and Advanced, 3 points. The number of languages known was graded in such a way that bilinguals scored 1 point and multilinguals scored 2 points. The respondents' level of English and their bilingualism or multilingualism (the independent variables) were correlated with the levels of awareness investigated in the questionnaire (the dependent variable). A two-tailed Kendall's tau, df = 511, was used at α decision level set at 0.05. Also, $2 \times 2 \chi^2$ tests were used to indicate differences between the groups of respondents. In addition, the research investigated the role of multilingualism in noticing the enhancing factor of cognate vocabulary in language learning. In a separate set of questions, the Multilinguals were asked to comment on the similarities between European languages they knew. Their answers were analysed with the use of qualitative methods.

Quantitative results: Multilinguals versus bilinguals

Question 1 (*Are Polish and English closely related?*) of the questionnaire (Appendix) focused on the perceptions of the typological distance between English and Polish. It turned out that the vast majority of students, with no regard to their knowledge of English and the number of languages known, did not perceive the two languages as such. Out of the 512 students questioned, 95% responded that the two languages were not closely related. As discussed above, psychotypological factors play a major role in noticing crosslinguistic similarities and may have manifold consequences for the learners' ability to use the possible affordances offered by cognate vocabulary. However, since Multilinguals and Bilinguals, without taking into account their level of English, were equally disadvantaged by their perception of the typological distance between English and Polish, this factor was excluded from the correlational analysis, since it did not differentiate the respondents.

In Question 5 of the questionnaire (Appendix), the respondents were asked to enumerate five cognates. Simple borrowings bearing high formal similarity to Polish (e.g. *radio*, *zebra* or *hamburger*) were assigned 1 point, whereas more sophisticated words of Latin and Greek origin (e.g. *intention* or *transcendental*) were assigned 2 points. The results are presented in Table 1.1.

A significant positive correlation was noted between the level of English and the types of cognates enumerated in this question ($\tau = 0.20$, $p < 0.01$), as well as between multilingualism and bilingualism and the types of cognates listed ($\tau = 0.24$, $p < 0.01$). On average, the lower the level of the respondents' English was, the simpler were the words they

Table 1.1 The number of students who enumerated the different types of cognates

	Elementary	Intermediate	Advanced	Multilingual
1-point cognates	65	87	93	29
2-point cognates	8	40	70	51
No answer	22	7	37	3
Total	95	134	200	83

enumerated. The Elementary students enumerated one- or two-syllable words, which were either recent borrowings into Polish or bore strong formal similarity to the relevant Polish items and could be found in course books for this level. The words listed by the Intermediate students were a mixture of simple items similar to those enumerated by the Elementary students, with some more sophisticated and longer words of Latin origin, or internationalisms. Interestingly, there were differences in the types of words listed by the Advanced and the Multilingual respondents, although numerous respondents in both these groups enumerated quite sophisticated items stemming from Latin or Greek. The 2×2 χ^2 tests showed significant differences between the Elementary and Intermediate respondents, $\chi^2(1) = 10.70$, $p < 0.001$, and between the Advanced and Multilingual respondents, $\chi^2(1) = 9.29$, $p < 0.002$. There was also a very small, but still significant, difference between the Intermediate and Advanced respondents, $\chi^2(1) = 3.97$, $p < 0.046$, in this respect.

The answers to Question 5 were positively correlated with the answers to Question 6 ($\tau = 0.36$, $p < 0.01$) and Question 7 ($\tau = 0.35$, $p < 0.01$). Question 6 (*How many words are there whose form and meaning are similar in English and Polish?*) of the questionnaire (Appendix) was meant to estimate how aware the respondents were of the number of English–Polish cognates available. Their answers were categorized and labelled: votes for below 150, low awareness; between 150 and 500, medium awareness; and above 500, high awareness of the existing cognates. The results for this question of the questionnaire are presented in Table 1.2 and Figure 1.1.

The results show that over half the Elementary respondents displayed low awareness of the existing cognates, and nearly 20% of them either could not answer or did not want to answer this question at all. About one-quarter of all the respondents showed medium awareness, whereas over half the Multilinguals proved to possess high awareness of the

Table 1.2 The respondents' answers to the question *How many words are there whose form and meaning are similar in English and Polish?*

Awareness	Elementary	Intermediate	Advanced	Multilinguals
Low	50	59	69	11
Medium	21	41	56	26
High	6	30	57	43
No answer	18	4	18	3
Total	95	134	200	83

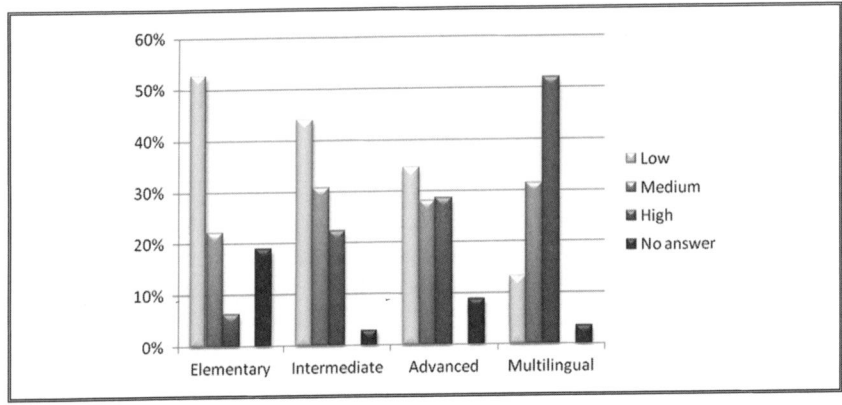

Figure 1.1 The respondents' awareness of the number of English–Polish cognates

cognates available. There is again an interesting discrepancy between the Advanced and the Multilingual respondents in this respect. For this question, significant positive correlations were noted between the levels of awareness and the level of English ($\tau = 0.25$, $p < 0.01$) and between the levels of awareness and bilingualism and multilingualism ($\tau = 0.27$, $p < 0.01$). In the next step, the awareness of cognates defined at two levels (no answer and low awareness/medium and high awareness) was compared between the groups of respondents. The χ^2 tests in the 2 × 2 scheme proved significant differences between the Elementary and Intermediate respondents, $\chi^2 (1) = 13.70$, $p < 0.001$, and between the Advanced and Multilingual respondents, $\chi^2 (1) = 18.13$, $p < 0.001$. However, there was no significant difference between the Intermediate and Advanced respondents, $\chi^2 (1) = 0.40$, $p < 0.53$, in this respect.

The low awareness of cognates displayed by bilinguals was even more evident in the case of Question 7 (*How many such words do YOU know?*; Appendix). The answers were also categorized and labelled: votes for circa 10 or circa 50, low awareness; circa 100, medium awareness; and circa 500 or more than 1000, high awareness. About 75% of the Elementary students and over 80% of the Intermediate students, as well as nearly 60% of the Advanced students examined displayed low awareness. On the other hand, nearly 70% of Multilinguals showed medium or high awareness. The answers to Questions 6 and 7 were strongly correlated ($\tau = 0.62$, $p < 0.01$). The detailed results are presented in Table 1.3 and in Figure 1.2 below.

A significant positive correlation was noted between the level of English and the levels of awareness displayed in this question ($\tau = 0.30$, $p < 0.01$), and a strong positive correlation was noted between multilingualism and

Table 1.3 The respondents' answers to the question *How many cognate words do YOU know?*

Awareness	Elementary	Intermediate	Advanced	Multilinguals
Low	70	109	119	24
Medium	5	15	39	29
High	0	4	15	25
No answer	20	6	27	5
Total	95	134	200	83

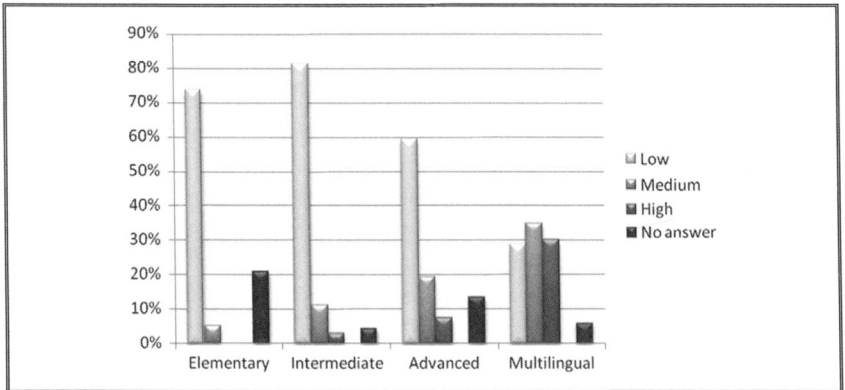

Figure 1.2 The respondents' awareness of the number of cognates in their lexicon

bilingualism and the levels of awareness ($\tau = 0.40$, $p < 0.01$). Similar to the previous question, in the next step, the awareness of cognates defined at two levels (no answer and low awareness/medium and high awareness) was compared between the groups of respondents. The χ^2 tests in the 2×2 scheme indicated a small but significant difference between the Elementary and Intermediate respondents, χ^2 (1) = 4.71, $p < 0.03$, and between the Intermediate and Advanced respondents, χ^2 (1) = 7.72, $p < 0.006$. The largest difference noted was again between the Advanced and Multilingual respondents, (χ^2 (1) = 36.01, $p < 0.001$.

Although it is quite clear that even the Advanced bilingual students were not fully aware of the potential of the cognate vocabulary they possessed, the Multilingual students proved to have a much higher awareness of crosslinguistic similarities. The answers of the Multilinguals clearly stood out from the answers of the remaining groups, including the Advanced, although their level of English and their language backgrounds were similar. The correlational analysis revealed that the level of awareness of cognates was more strongly interrelated with multilingualism than with the level of advancement in English. Thus, in accordance with the assumption that the awareness of cognates influences the range of affordances available to the learner, it is possible to state that the Multilingual respondents had a wider range of affordances at their disposal. The results clearly show that the first threshold in noticing such affordances is the level of the learner's L2, whereas the second threshold is the command of more than two languages.

Qualitative results: Affordances Noticed by Multilinguals

The Multilinguals were additionally asked to answer five questions concerning their perception of similarities between the European languages they knew: *Do you notice any considerable similarities between the European languages you know? Which language systems are the most similar? Do the similarities help you in language learning? What helps the most?* The questions were formulated in Polish. In addition, they were asked to comment on any regularities they noticed concerning the lexical similarities between European languages. The answers leave no doubt that the Multilinguals perceived searching for crosslinguistic similarities, particularly in the area of lexis, as an important and useful strategy in language learning.

A great majority of the Multilingual respondents (89%) admitted noticing considerable similarities between the European languages they used. Of the systems (grammar, vocabulary or phonology), 68% of students chose vocabulary as the most similar across European languages, 31% chose grammar and only 1% phonology. This may be because all the multilingual respondents had done courses in phonetics and phonology of the languages they studied. These courses usually aim at improving the learners' pronunciation by pointing to the differences between the language studied and their native Polish. The Multilinguals strongly agreed that crosslinguistic similarities helped them with language learning (95% positive answers) and strongly pointed to lexical similarities (64%) as the most helpful. Interestingly enough, they did not see phonological similarities as relevant for language learning.

The Multilinguals were also asked to comment on the regularities concerning the lexical similarities between European languages. Altogether, 77 commentaries were obtained, with only one student claiming not to notice any regularity. The comments, all in Polish, were often long and sophisticated: they revealed the students' considerable linguistic and metalinguistic awareness, although many of the respondents did not use metalanguage when commenting. Half the Multilinguals pointed to the influence of Latin and Greek (42 comments) on the European languages. One-third of the respondents mentioned the common roots of languages and language families (20 comments), as well as the historical processes of language change, including the process of borrowing (14 comments). A considerable number among the Multilinguals commented on similarities in specialist vocabulary (17 comments). Finally, the students pointed to morphological similarities (11 comments). Four students additionally commented on the learning process and stylistic issues:

- *Im lepiej zna się język, tym więcej podobieństw się dostrzega* (The better you know the language, the more similarities you notice).
- *Zauważyłam, ze zwiększając swój zasób słów języka polskiego poszerzam również zakres rozumianych słów języków obcych* (I have noticed that expanding my Polish vocabulary helps me understand a wider range of foreign words).
- *Według mnie najwięcej podobnych słów jest typowych dla języka formalnego, bardziej eleganckiego niż codzienny* (According to me, a large number of cognate words are typical of formal language, more elegant than everyday language).
- *Łatwiej przyswaja się kolejne słowa nowego języka, gdy występowały podobne we wcześniej poznanym języku.* (It is easier to acquire words in the new language if there are similar words in the language you already know).

The comments presented above show that the Multilinguals, who are proficient in several languages, acknowledge the existence of cross-linguistic similarities in the area of lexis and can use the potential affordances such similarities offer. This remains in accordance with Singleton and Aronin who stated that

> [...] multilinguals have a more extensive range of affordances available to them than other language users and [...] their experience as multilinguals provides them with especially favourable conditions to develop awareness of the social and cognitive possibilities which their situation affords them. (Singleton & Aronin 2007: 83)

Conclusions and Implications for Language Teaching

The present chapter briefly outlined the theory of affordances and its importance for second language acquisition. It showed that language learners have certain potential affordances at their disposal and that learning languages successfully depends on the language learner's capacity to perceive and utilize the linguistic affordances embedded in the studying environment. The chapter discussed the fact that thousands of cognate words in the European languages, even as typologically distant as Polish and English, may offer a set of affordances to the learner who is aware of their existence. The awareness depends on language typology and psychotypology, the language level of the learner and whether they are bilingual or multilingual.

The survey conducted on Polish learners of English showed that a vast majority of all the students examined perceived Polish and English as typologically distant and that most bilingual respondents were not aware of the existence of cognates. It was also shown that the ability to notice cognate relationships depended on the learners' level of L2. The students at lower levels paid attention only to formal similarities, and they did not automatically assume the existence of more numerous and varied types of cognates. This proves support for the first hypothesis of a positive relationship between the level of English and the awareness of cognates. However, it was surprising to find that even advanced bilingual learners of English were unaware of the cognates that they obviously knew and used, as word listing had proved. Despite the growth of awareness connected with the language level, most bilingual students underestimated the number of cognates in their own lexicon. On the other hand, the awareness of cognates positively correlated with multilingualism. Of the students examined, only multilingual learners proficient in several languages tended to notice cognates and make conscious use of them as a learning strategy, as shown by the quantitative and qualitative results. Therefore, it is possible to claim that, as far as Polish–English lexical crosslinguistic similarities are concerned, only the multilingual students examined possessed and used a wide range of affordances offered by a cognate vocabulary. The study corroborated the second research hypothesis concerning a positive relationship between multilingualism and the awareness of cognates.

The research findings have several implications for language teaching. Generally, the lower the level of the bilingual learners' English is, the lower is their awareness of lexical similarities. Since English is used as a *lingua franca* throughout Europe, this is an important signal for teachers and syllabus designers. It is not difficult to notice that Latin- and Greek-based words are quite common in formal styles and registers used by educated European speakers in their L1 (c.f. the comments by the Multilinguals). Unfortunately, such words are typically taught relatively late in English language courses since, according to Dörnyei and Skehan (2003: 593), syllabus designers assume that learners are essentially homogeneous. However, while the word *optimistic* may be difficult for learners of various language backgrounds, it is not for speakers of those languages that borrowed from Latin in the past. Thus, activating such a word can take place even at the beginning of a language course for educated European learners. In the light of the research presented, one can claim that, in the case of most European languages, training students to recognize and make conscious use of crosslinguistic lexical similarities should enhance the learning process and help them notice the potential affordances such similarities offer. However, awareness training must be preceded by producing more L1-specific teaching materials to be used alongside course books (e.g. the EuroCom Project for typologically close languages; Hufeisen & Marx, 2007).

Apart from creating new teaching materials, it is also worth appreciating the role of the teacher who is aware of the potential language affordances. As Tella and Harjanne (2007: 503, original emphasis) put it, '[t]he language teacher must also be fluent in this "language" [of potential affordances] so as to design tasks that *tell the pupils* why to work on them and how to do it in the most beneficial way'. Thus, not only the learners' roles but also the teachers' roles in the language classroom should change. Only those teachers who are aware of linguistic affordances will be able to help learners notice them. A teacher who is aware of affordances offered by crosslinguistic similarities should understand the role of the learners' language backgrounds and should be able to make comparisons with the languages the students already use. So, it seems reasonable to postulate introducing awareness-raising not only to language teaching but also to teacher training.

Acknowledgements

I thank my anonymous reviewers for their valuable comments. I want to express my deep gratitude to two people without whom this chapter would not have been written: Dr Larissa Aronin for helping me believe in myself and Professor Maciej Haman for making me appreciate the beauty and elegance of statistical analysis.

References

Barwise, J. and Perry, J. (1983) *Situations and Attitudes*. Cambridge: MIT-Bradford.

Cenoz, J. and Genesse, F. (1998) Psycholinguistic perspectives on multilingualism and multilingual education. In J. Cenoz and F. Genesse (eds) *Beyond Bilingualism: Multilingualism and Multilingual Education* (pp. 16–32). Clevedon: Multilingual Matters.

Cenoz, J., Hufeisen, B. and Jessner, U. (eds) (2001) *Cross-linguistic Influence in Third Language Acquisition: Psycholinguistic Perspectives*. Clevedon: Multilingual Matters.

Dörnyei, Z. and Skehan, P. (2003) Individual differences in second language learning. In C. Doughty and M. Long (eds) *The Handbook of Second Language Acquisition* (pp. 589–630). Oxford: Blackwell.

Duškova, L. (1984) Similarity – an aid or hindrance in foreign language learning? *Folia Linguistica* 18, 103–115.

Gass, S. (1997) *Input, Interaction and the Second Language Learner.* Mahwah, NJ: Erlbaum.

Gass, S., Svetics, I. and Lemelin, S. (2003) Differential effects of attention. *Language Learning* 53 (3), 497–545.

Gibson, J.J. (1977) The theory of affordances. In R.E. Shaw and J. Bransford (eds) *Perceiving, Acting, and Knowing.* Hillsdale, NJ: Erlbaum.

Gibson, J.J. (1979) *The Ecological Approach to Visual Perception.* Boston: Houghton Mifflin.

Haastrup, K. (1991) *Lexical Inferencing Procedures or Talking about Words: A Book about Receptive Procedures in Foreign Language Learning with Special Reference to English.* Tübingen: Gunter Narr.

Herdina, P. and Jessner, U. (2002) *A Dynamic Model of Multilingualism: Perspectives of Change in Psycholinguistics.* Clevedon: Multilingual Matters.

Hoffmann, C. (2001) The status of trilingualism in bilingual studies. In J. Cenoz, B. Hufeisen and U. Jessner (eds) *Looking Beyond Second Language Acquisition: Studies in Tri- and Multilingualism* (pp. 13–25). Tübingen: Stauffenburg.

Hufeisen, B. and Marx, N. (2007) *EuroComGerm – Die Sieben Siebe: Germanische Sprachen lesen lernen.* Aachen: Shaker Verlag.

Jessner, U. (1999) Metalinguistic awareness in multilinguals: Cognitive aspects of third language learning [Electronic version]. *Language Awareness* 8 (3–4), 201–209.

Jessner, U. (2008) Teaching third languages: Findings, trends and challenges [Electronic version]. *Language Teaching* 41 (1), 15–56.

Kellerman, E. (1977) Towards a characterization of the strategy of transfer in second language learning. *International Studies Bulletin* 2, 58–145.

Kellerman, E. (1983) Now you see it, now you don't. In S. Gass and L. Selinker (eds) *Language Transfer in Language Learning* (pp. 112–134). Rowley, MA: Newbury House.

Macnamara, J. (1967) The bilingual's linguistic performance: A psychological overview. *Journal of Social Issues* 23, 59–77.

MacWhinney, B. (1999) The emergence of language from embodiment. In B. MacWhinney (ed.) *The Emergence of Language* (pp. 213–256). Mahwah, NJ: Erlbaum.

Nation, P. and Meara, P. (2002) Vocabulary. In N. Schmitt (ed.) *An Introduction to Applied Linguistics* (pp. 35–53). London: Arnold.

Norman, D.A. (1988) *The Psychology of Everyday Things.* New York: Basic Books.

Norman, D.A. (1999) Affordances, conventions and design. *Interactions* 6 (3), 38–43.

Odlin, T. (1989) *Language Transfer.* Cambridge: Cambridge University Press.

Odlin, T. (2002) Language transfer and cross-linguistic studies: Relativism, universalism, and the native language. In R.B. Kaplan (ed.) *The Oxford Handbook of Applied Linguistics* (pp. 253–261). Oxford: Oxford University Press.

Odlin, T. (2003) Cross-linguistic influence. In C. Doughty and M. Long (eds) *The Handbook of Second Language Acquisition* (pp. 436–486). Oxford: Blackwell.

Odlin, T. (2006) Could a contrastive analysis ever be complete? In J. Arabski (ed.) *Cross-linguistic Influences in the Second Language Lexicon* (pp. 22–35). Clevedon: Multilingual Matters.

Otwinowska-Kasztelanic, A. (2001) *A Study of the Lexico-Semantic and Grammatical Influence of English on the Polish of the Younger Generation of Poles (19–35 Years of Age).* Warszawa: Wydawnictwo Akademickie Dialog.

Otwinowska-Kasztelanic, A. (2007) Positive transfer and motivation in teaching cognate vocabulary. In J. Arabski (ed.) *Challenging Tasks for Psycholinguistics in the New Century* (pp. 613–621). Katowice: Wydawnictwo Uniwersytetu Śląskiego.

Otwinowska-Kasztelanic, A. (2009) Raising awareness of cognate vocabulary as a strategy in teaching English to Polish adults. *Innovation in Language Learning and Teaching* 3 (2), 131–148.

Otwinowska-Kasztelanic, A. (2010) Language awareness in using cognate vocabulary: The case of Polish advanced students of English in the light of the theory of affordances. In J. Arabski and A. Wojtaszek (eds) *Neurolinguistic and Psycholinguistic Perspectives on SLA* (pp. 175–190). Bristol: Multilingual Matters.

Ringbom, H. (1986) Crosslinguistic influence and foreign language learning process. In E. Kellerman and M. Sharwood-Smith (eds) *Crosslinguistic Influence in Second Language Acquisition* (pp. 150–162). New York: Pergamon.

Ringbom, H. (1987) *The Role of the First Language in Foreign Language Learning*. Clevedon: Multilingual Matters.

Ringbom, H. (2006) The importance of different types of similarity in transfer studies. In J. Arabski (ed.) *Cross-linguistic Influences in the Second Language Lexicon* (pp. 36–45). Clevedon: Multilingual Matters.

Ringbom, H. (2007) *Cross-linguistic Similarity in Foreign Language Learning*. Clevedon: Multilingual Matters.

Rusiecki, J. (2002) Friends true and false. A contrastive approach to the lexicon. In J. Arabski (ed.) *Time for Words* (pp. 71–81). Frankfurt-am-Main: Peter Lang.

Schmidt, R. (1990) The role of consciousness in second language learning. *Applied Linguistics* 11, 129–158.

Schmidt, R. (1998) The centrality of attention in SLA. *University of Hawaii Working Papers in ESL* 16, 1–34.

Schmidt, R. (2001) Attention. In P. Robomson (ed.) *Cognition and Second Language Instruction* (pp. 3–32). Cambridge: Cambridge University Press.

Schmitt, N. (1997) Vocabulary learning strategies. In N. Schmitt and M. McCarthy (eds) *Vocabulary. Description, Acquisition and Pedagogy* (pp. 199–227). Cambridge: Cambridge University Press.

Schumann, J. (1997) *The Neurobiology of Affect in Language*. Malden, MA: Blackwell.

Segalowitz, N. (1997) Individual differences in second language acquisition. In A. de Groot and J.F. Kroll (eds) *Tutorials in Bilingualism: Psycholinguistic Perspectives* (pp. 85–112). Mahwah, NJ: Erlbaum.

Segalowitz, N. (2001) On the evolving connections between psychology and linguistics [Electronic version]. *Annual Review of Applied Linguistics* 21, 3–22.

Singleton, D. (2006) Lexical transfer: Interlexical or intralexical? In J. Arabski (ed.) *Cross-linguistic Influences in the Second Language Lexicon* (pp. 130–143). Clevedon: Multilingual Matters.

Singleton, D. and Aronin L. (2007) Multiple language learning in the light of the theory of affordances. *Innovation in Language Learning and Teaching* 1 (1), 83–96.

Swan, M. (1997) The influence of the mother tongue on second language vocabulary acquisition and use. In N. Schmitt and M. McCarthy (eds) *Vocabulary. Description, Acquisition and Pedagogy* (pp. 156–180). Cambridge: Cambridge University Press.

Tella, S. and Harjanne, P. (2007) Can we afford any more affordances? Foreign language education specific reflections. In K. Teoksessa, K. Merenluoto, A. Virta and P. Carpelan (eds) *Opettajankoulutuksen muuttuvat rakenteet. Ainedidaktinen symposium 9.2.2007. Turun opettajankoulutuslaitos*, 500–506. On WWW at http://www.helsinki.fi/ ~ tella/ads07.pdf. Accessed 20.11.08.

van Lier, L. (2000) From input to affordance: Social-interactive learning from an ecological perspective. In J.P. Lantolf (ed.) *Sociocultural Theory and Second Language Learning* (pp. 245–259). Oxford: Oxford University Press.

Wode, H. (1983) On the systematicity of L1 transfer in L2 acquisition. In H. Wode (ed.) *Papers on Language Acquisition, Language Learning and Language Teaching* (pp. 144–149). Heidelberg: J. Groos Verlag.

Appendix

Questionnaire for Polish learners of English (English language version)

Please choose one answer.

1. Are Polish and English closely related?
   (a) Yes   (b) No

2. Which systems of English are the most similar to Polish?
   (a) Grammar   (b) Vocabulary   (c) Phonology

3. Which systems of English are the easiest to master for a Pole?
   (a) Grammar   (b) Vocabulary   (c) Phonology

4. When is it easier to understand a written text?
   (a) When you know   (b) When you understand
       grammar well   vocabulary well

5. List five cognates (i.e. words whose form and meaning are similar in English and Polish).
   ....
   ....
   ....
   ....
   ....

6. How many such cognate words are there?
   (a) 20–50   (b) 50–150   (c) 150–500   (d) 500–1000   (e) 1000–5000

7. How many such words do YOU know?
   (a) ca 10   (b) ca 50   (c) ca 100   (d) ca 500   (e) more than 1000

Chapter 2

Perceived Redundancy or Crosslinguistic Influence? What L3 Learners' Material Can Tell us About the Causes of Errors

HÅKAN RINGBOM

In Finland, there has been a change in priority in the choice of language in school during the last 30 years. Although Finnish speakers previously started with Swedish as their first foreign language learned in school, more than 90% of them now start with English, which is a much more popular language than Swedish with young people. Thus, for most Finns today, English is the L2 and Swedish is the L3, although the order was generally reversed before the 80s. Either way, the formal similarities between the non-native language and the target language (TL) have been shown to have considerable influence from a non-native L2, at least at the lexical level. Transfer, however, seems to be just one of the strategies learners use to cope with problems in producing and learning a TL. For language learners in the early stages, one important strategy is the opposition to what is perceived as redundancy in the TL (George, 1972). This means that the learner imposes his own naïve standards of efficiency in order to facilitate the learning task in the early stages of learning. A natural tendency for learners in their production is to omit elements perceived as redundant on the basis of prior knowledge.

Opposition to redundancy can be found in L1 learning, L2 learning and L3 learning. All natural languages have redundancies, and an important task of the learner is to cope with these redundancies in a way similar to native speakers. It is well known that when children learn their L1, they frequently, at one stage, produce forms such as *runned* and *goed* instead of *ran* and *went*. The child has learnt how past tense is normally expressed but not the exceptions, which according to his thinking, show unnecessary redundancy. Overgeneralization of the rule of forming past tense involves a refusal to accept more than one way of expressing past tense (i.e. opposition to redundancy). The child's naïve but logical reaction is to regard the irregular forms of the past as redundant and to use the regular endings. This naïve standard of efficiency cannot, in the long run, persist against the pressure to conform to adult standards (i.e. the child gradually learns to cope with redundancy).

Probably the only researcher dealing at any length with the learner's avoidance of redundancy in the TL is George (1972). For him, it is redundancy, not transfer, which is in focus for the learner. As he says, 'A knowledge of the learners' mother tongue is necessary so that one becomes aware of their perception, not of the differences between their mother tongue and English, but rather of the redundancy of English' (George, 1972: 45). His work must be seen against the background of the negative attitudes towards transfer in the early 70s, when 'transfer' was commonly regarded as a dirty word since it was associated with the strongly criticized structuralist and behaviourist views of language. In line with most of his contemporaries, George viewed transfer as something exclusively negative or as interference. One important reason for this mistaken view is that transfer, in his thinking, was based on linguistic differences between the TL and L1. However, this is not the case: Learners are primarily concerned not with differences but with similarities. What is important for learners is not what linguistic differences there are between the TL and L1 but whether they can perceive similarities and relate these to prior knowledge. The use they make of these similarities, sometimes perceived, sometimes merely assumed, reflect transfer.

In the early stages of learning, Finnish L2 learners of English have frequently been found to omit prepositions and articles since these grammatical categories do not exist in their L1 and are, therefore, perceived to be redundant in the TL English. For the same reason, English or Swedish learners of Finnish often omit many of the 14 case endings of Finnish nouns since these cases are perceived to be redundant, that is, not present in their L1. Further, English learners of Swedish, even at relatively advanced stages, often make the error of leaving the adjective uninflected, when it should conform to the number and gender of the noun it qualifies.

In L3 learning, the learner has the chance to rely not just on one but on two languages – two different forms of prior knowledge. What choice the learner makes greatly depends on psychotypology (see Kellerman, 1995): Which language is perceived to be more similar to the TL, L3? Learners perceive English to be similar to Swedish, whereas few concrete similarities are perceived between English and Finnish. There are structural aspects where the three languages differ considerably from each other, and I will take as relevant examples the noun phrase (NP) and the second person personal and possessive pronouns.

Table 2.1 details the different structures of the NP in Swedish, English and Finnish:

Finnish NPs have a complex structure in that there are 14 productive cases of the noun (some say 15 or 16) and both the noun and the adjective are declined for case and number. There is no marking of the distinction between definite and indefinite, which is often indicated by word order

Table 2.1 The structure of the noun phrase

	Swedish (L3)	English (L2)	Finnish (L1)
Nouns	5 declinations; plural endings -ar, -er, -or, -(e)n,-zero; suffix def. article -(e)n, -na	No declinations; definite & indef. article, no suffix article	14 productive cases in sg. and plural; no articles
Adjectives	Declined for number and gender (fin, fint, fina)	Undeclined	Declined for case & number (14 cases in sg. and pl.)
Extended NP (indef.)	Article + attribute + noun (en fin middag fina middagar)	Plural indicated only in nouns (a fine dinner, fine dinners)	Declined for case and number (no marking of indef.) (hieno päivällinen hienot päivälliset, hienoissa päivällisissä (= in the fine dinners))
Extended NP (def.)	Double marking of definiteness **den** fina middag**en** **de** fina middag**arna**	Def. article; uninflected adj. the fine dinner the fine dinners	Declined for case and number; no marking of definiteness (hieno päivällinen hienot päivälliset)

alone (*oven edessä on auto – auto on oven edessä* corresponds to 'a car is in front of the door' – 'the car is in front of the door'). English and Swedish both have only one inflected case of the noun as well as a system of definite and indefinite articles, but English NPs have a much simpler structure in that there is only one plural ending of the noun and the adjective is always left undeclined.

Swedish occupies a middle position between Finnish and English. It has five different declinations of the noun. The adjectives can also take many different forms. They are declined for number and gender, taking the plural ending **-a,** and a particularly tricky point for learners is the double marking of definiteness in extended NPs (**den** fina middag**en** (sg.), **de** fina middag**arna** (pl.).

In a recent study, learners' use of Swedish NPs was analysed by Heikkilä (2008). She studied the Swedish of Finnish cadets training to be officers at a military school. They have a fair knowledge of English, but their Swedish is generally at a very elementary level. One interesting finding in Heikkilä's material is that the learners show the tendency to leave out the suffix article needed in extended NPs. When learners were asked to translate 'the most recent course' (Fi. *nuorin kurssi,* which in Swedish should be written as '**den** yngsta kursen'), 29% (374 out of 1070

Table 2.2 Second person pronouns in Swedish, English and Finnish

	Sw. L3	Eng. L2	Fi. L1
Pers. 2 p.sg.	du	you	sinä
Pers. 2 p. pl.	ni	you	te
Pers. 2 p. sg. obj.	dig	you	sinut
Pers. 2 p. pl. obj.	er	you	teidät
Poss. 2 p. sg.	din, ditt, dina	your	sinun
Poss. 2 p. pl.	er, ert, era	your	teidän

instances) omitted the obligatory suffix article. In Heikkilä's corpus of free production, she found that the percentage was even larger: out of 149 extended NPs used, there were 56 omissions of the suffix article (38%). Heikkilä's Finnish learners consistently simplified the structure of the extended NPs in Swedish. They seem to perceive the suffix ending as redundant, since there is already an article indicating definiteness. They have learnt that definiteness is expressed by a preposed article in Swedish, but in their construction of the extended NP, they stick to the simpler English pattern, where there is no additional suffix ending.

The personal pronouns follow a similar pattern. English has a simpler system in this respect, whereas the Swedish system is more complex. The three languages have the following system of personal pronouns, as shown in Table 2.2.

Swedish and Finnish have a similar, rather complex, pattern, whereas English has a much simpler pattern. Heikkilä's cadets frequently overgeneralize one form, *du*, using it where some other form should have been used:

Examples:

Translation of Fi. Oletteko kuulleet? (= have you (pl.) heard?)

101 subjects: ni 50% (correct)
               du 44%

Translation of Fi. Voimme kertoa teille (= we can tell you (pl.))

er   21% (correct)
dig 28%
ni   10%

du	6%
Others	23%
Omissions	11%

Source: Heikkilä (2008: 63)

Should we then try to establish in detail whether the learners in each case perceived redundancy on the basis of the Swedish pattern or whether their constructions reflected crosslinguistic influence from L2 English? I think this would be a futile task.

My point here is that these are much the same thing, since both transfer and opposition to redundancy ultimately go back to the same assumption by the learner: that the TL should be similar to prior knowledge of another language. We can, in fact, say that opposition to redundancy reflects crosslinguistic influence at a covert level, much in the same way as avoidance of certain TL constructions does. Opposition to perceived redundancy can be regarded as a subset of crosslinguistic influence from L1 or from L2. Prior knowledge provides a standard for the assessment of redundancy in the TL, and the learner's assumptions may or may not be correct. In more general terms, we may also see the opposition to redundancy as a subconscious attempt in learners to reduce their workload in order to facilitate their learning. Thus, not only can L1 serve as a basis for perceiving redundancy in the TL, but a good knowledge of L2 can do that as well. In Heikkilä's material, more similarities are perceived between L3 and L2 than between L3 and L1. English and Swedish are perceived to be similar in many respects, and as Jarvis and Pavlenko (2008: 180) say, '[A] characteristic of perceived similarities is that, once they cross a certain threshold, they tend to lead the learner to assume additional similarities – even ones that do not actually exist between the languages'. This brings up the difference between perceived and assumed similarities, which has been treated in two recent works, Jarvis and Pavlenko (2008) and Ringbom (2007) (c.f. also Ringbom and Jarvis, 2009). As Jarvis and Pavlenko say:

> A perceived similarity is a conscious or unconscious judgment that a form, structure, meaning, function or pattern that an L2 user has encountered in the input of the recipient language is similar to a corresponding feature in the source language. An assumed similarity, on the other hand, is a conscious or unconscious hypothesis that a form, structure, meaning, function or pattern that exists in the source language has a counterpart in the recipient language, regardless of whether the L2 user has yet encountered anything like it in the recipient language and regardless of whether it actually does exist in the recipient language. Now, to be clear, perceived and assumed

similarities are not always mutually exclusive. In fact, they represent a set–subset relationship in that all perceived similarities are also assumed similarities, but not all assumed similarities are actually perceived. (Jarvis & Pavlenko, 2008: 179)

Jarvis and Pavlenko also comment on the differences between positive and negative transfer: 'Positive transfer occurs when assumed similarities are compatible with objective similarities, whereas negative transfer occurs when assumed similarities conflict with objective differences' (Jarvis & Pavlenko, 2008: 182; see also Ringbom & Jarvis, 2009). Although recent works such as Jarvis and Pavlenko's important book have contributed more knowledge about the processes and strategies of learning, we should not forget that earlier scholars, such as George, also made worthwhile observations in the area. One aim of this paper is to call attention to George's book (1972), even though it is almost 40 years old. One of George's shortcomings is his reluctance to consider crosslinguistic influence since he, like most of his contemporary linguists, tended to regard the L1 as merely an obstacle to learning, not an aid. All the same, George makes a number of perceptive remarks on the learning and teaching of foreign languages, and it is well worth taking a closer look at his book. It was written within an outdated research paradigm, and it should be brought into a different theoretical framework of various types of crosslinguistic influence. If this is done, perceived redundancy is a useful concept, providing an additional focus on how learners approach the task of learning a new language.

References

George, H.V. (1972) *Common Errors in Language Learning*. Rowley, MA: Newbury House.
Heikkilä. T-L. (2008) *Engelskans inflytande på nominalfrasen i finskspråkiga kadetters svenska*. Helsingfors: Försvarshögskolan.
Jarvis, S. and Pavlenko, A. (2008) *Crosslinguistic Influence in Language and Cognition*. New York: Routledge.
Kellerman, E. (1995) Crosslinguistic influence: Transfer to nowhere? *Annual Review of Applied Linguistics* 15, 125–150.
Ringbom, H. (2007) *Cross-linguistic Similarity in Foreign Language Learning*. Clevedon: Multilingual Matters.
Ringbom, H. and Jarvis, S. (2009) The importance of cross-linguistic similarity in foreign language learning. In M.H. Long and C.J. Doughty (eds) *The Handbook of Language Teaching*. Malden, MA: Wiley-Blackwell.

Chapter 3
Crosslinguistic Interaction and Metalinguistic Awareness in Third Language Acquisition

MARIANA BONO

Introduction

The specific nature of third or additional language acquisition[1] (TLA) is now well established, and important research has been carried out in the last decade to account for the roles of second languages in the acquisition of a third language and the significance of metalinguistic awareness in this process. The crosslinguistic and metalinguistic dimensions of TLA are closely intertwined, and we will argue that a full account of multilinguals' specific competencies needs to take both into consideration.

By virtue of their extended linguistic repertoire, multilingual learners do not have one but several source languages at their disposal. Multiple sources inevitably lead to complex, dynamic and multidirectional crosslinguistic interplay, with native and non-native languages playing different roles. Several publications have investigated the specific influence of non-native languages in the acquisition process (Cenoz *et al.*, 2001, 2003; Rast & Trévisiol, 2006; De Angelis, 2007; Hammarberg, 2009, *inter alia*). The study of crosslinguistic interaction (CLIN) can be approached from different theoretical and empirical perspectives, but the examination of language switches that involve an L2 rather than the L1 is a preferred option for reasons that we will discuss here. Overall, significant progress has been made towards an understanding of L2 influence on L3 acquisition and the factors that condition the learner's reliance on prior L2 knowledge. Two issues, however, require further investigation: (1) the extent to which learners are able to analyse and monitor CLIN and (2) its true potential as a learning asset. In other words, are multilingual learners aware of CLIN phenomena, and most importantly, are they able to exploit crosslinguistic associations in the learning process?

It is difficult to provide straightforward answers to these questions. The analysis of multilinguals' speech production shows that prior L2 knowledge does not always translate into conscious learning or communicative strategies. On the contrary, a significant number of language switches, particularly L3–L2 switches, seem to be unintentional. Whatever the level of consciousness underlying transfer operations, the sources of transfer are hard to pinpoint and, needless to say, learners may or may not be able to offer an explanation for their linguistic behaviour. Think-aloud protocols have been shown to effectively encourage learners to do so, but gaining access to the mental processes and representations involved in crosslinguistic comparison remains a considerable challenge for researchers who work in multilingual settings. For those with an interest in the learning outcomes of multilingualism, it is equally difficult to assess the extent to which knowledge of two or several languages can foster further language acquisition. Considering learners' failure to identify L2 influence as such (documented in De Angelis, 2005), it could be argued that CLIN is both inevitable and undesirable. It is true that increased opportunities for establishing crosslinguistic comparisons do not necessarily result in a perceived cognitive gain and that – regardless of the degree of typological proximity – some learners may actually resent, and thus attempt to neutralise, the influence of their non-native languages (Bono, 2007, 2008b). To complicate matters further, the analyst dealing with oral data can only identify the language switches that result in non-target forms. 'Successful' transfer operations – that is, transfer that enables the learner to accurately understand or produce L3 linguistic units – often go unseen.

In this chapter, we argue that, despite the widespread perception among certain learners that their languages compete among each other and are, therefore, best kept apart, the possibility to establish crosslinguistic associations based on the similarities or differences between known languages is a powerful tool that can be turned to the learner's advantage *if certain conditions are met*. The hypothesis will be raised here that for L2 influence to become a learning accelerator, CLIN needs to be coupled with metalinguistic awareness, which is known to be particularly enhanced in multilingual speakers.

In the next section, we review the relevant literature and delineate a theoretical framework for the study of the crosslinguistic and metalinguistic dimensions in TLA. The majority of publications that will be mentioned, in this chapter, deal with language acquisition in formal settings. In line with our own research agenda, special attention will be paid to studies that undertake to account for CLIN phenomena in spontaneous speech production. A note of caution needs to be made regarding the type of multilingualism that is being considered for study. Our interest is in formal language learning. In our research as well as in most of the works that are discussed here, it is usually possible to clearly identify and separate the L1, acquired in early childhood, from the L2 and other non-native languages (L3, L4, L5 ...) acquired after the critical period, usually in a school environment. We acknowledge that early bilingualism and naturalistic language learning raise different questions, for instance, regarding the status of languages within the learner's repertoire, but these will not be addressed in this chapter.

Section 3 provides a description of the empirical study, including the research design and methodology, the participants and the data and the analytical categories that have been used.

Section 4 is divided into four parts. In the first two parts we present and discuss our general findings regarding the number and function of the language switches identified in small group conversations in Spanish. We focus specifically on lexical inserts in order to discuss the source languages (or 'supplier languages'). The third and fourth parts are devoted to the analysis of verbal evidence of underlying metalinguistic activity. We describe and analyse two different phenomena: on the one hand, we discuss language switches, generally involving more than one word, which are metalinguistically driven; on the other hand, we present conversational data that bear traces of a crosslinguistic comparison or association without necessarily triggering a language switch.

Section 5 provides further elements of discussion, considers alternative research methods and sums up the results of our present study.

Review of the Literature

Crosslinguistic influence in third language acquisition

CLIN and transfer phenomena, in particular, are well documented in second-language acquisition (SLA) research (Gass & Selinker, 1983, 1994; Kellerman & Sharwood Smith, 1986). Traditionally, mainstream SLA studies approach transfer as a synonym for native language influence (e.g. Ellis, 1994: 11) and adopt a 'no-difference' assumption based on the premise that the processes underlying the acquisition of all non-native languages are essentially the same (De Angelis, 2007). However, notes of caution regarding the open-ended semantics of the term 'second' in SLA were raised as early as the 1980s. As far as transfer mechanisms are concerned, in his book *Language Transfer,* Odlin referred to the overwhelming tendency to equate *transfer* and *L1 influence* as a 'convenient fiction' that failed to portray the whole picture for multilingual learners:

> When individuals know two languages, knowledge of both may affect the acquisition of a third. Most probably, knowledge of three or more languages can lead to three or more different kinds of source language influence, although pinning down the exact influences in multilingual situations is often hard. (Odlin, 1989: 27)

The hypothesis that non-native languages can play a part in the acquisition process was not altogether absent from the literature, but it was usually expressed parenthetically and presented as a peripheral, anecdotal issue. 'Clearly what the learner knows of a language (his mother tongue and any other languages he has) is part of the learning device itself'; this statement by Corder (1981: 58) illustrates this trend, as do his comments on the role of non-native languages in his seminal article, *A role for the mother tongue*:

> [...] where one of these other second languages is formally more closely related to the target language, borrowing is preferred from that language rather than from the mother tongue. It sometimes appears the case that there is a positive preference for borrowing from other second languages, and often the less well known they are to the learner the more they prove a source of borrowing. Needless to say, these processes are by no means always conscious or even accessible to introspection, but *it does seem from anecdotal evidence that the mother tongue is perceived to be more different than it often in fact is, and that the other second languages are perceived, perhaps erroneously, to be linguistically more close to the target language.* The mother tongue does appear to have some sort of unique status. (Corder, 1983: 94, italics ours)

These early observations about the possible role of non-native languages in further language learning coupled with growing interest among researchers about language acquisition *beyond* the L2 paved the way for a true change of focus and eventually led to the emergence of TLA studies as an independent field (De Angelis & Dewaele, 2009). Multiple CLINs are now regarded as a central component in the theoretical models that account for the specificity of TLA. The research agenda includes the unique status of the L1 in the multilingual repertoire, real versus perceived typological distance and the different kinds of source language influence in TLA (Clyne, 1997, 2003; Coste, 2001; Cenoz et al., 2001, 2003; De Angelis, 2007; Hammarberg, 2009; Herdina & Jessner, 2002; Hufeisen & Lindemann, 1998; Rast & Trévisiol, 2006; Ringbom, 2007).

With regards to all these issues, there is a fundamental continuity between the research work carried on transfer and other crosslinguistic phenomena in SLA in the late 1970s and early 1980s and current research on TLA. In particular, to understand CLIN in L3 learning, researchers draw on early work on the factors that constrain linguistic transfer. By way of example, the notion of *psychotypology*, devised by Kellerman (1978, 1979, 1983) to account for the difference between real and perceived typological distance, has remained central to most accounts of the impact of CLIN in the learning process, and there is nowadays general agreement that crosslinguistic distance as perceived and evaluated by the learner impacts the transferability of linguistic features from one language to another.

Notwithstanding the 'natural' evolution from SLA to TLA, recent theoretical developments have definitively brought into question the non-difference assumption in SLA (De Angelis, 2007 and *supra*). The L1 may remain an important source of influence when learning a L3, but we now know that

- other known languages can play an even more important role (Coste, 2001; Clyne, 1997, 2003; De Angelis, 2005; Rast, in press; Ringbom, 2007);
- different languages may compete for selection at a single point in time (De Angelis & Selinker, 2001) and
- different languages feature different levels of activation, and the L1 is not necessarily always the dominant active language (Dewaele, 1998).

We will now comment on the study carried out by Williams and Hammarberg, which has greatly contributed to build such a consensus. The authors investigated language switches in the speech production of an adult learner of Swedish L3 (Hammarberg & Williams, 1993, 1998; see also Hammarberg, 2001, 2006). The results of their case study indicate that the learner's L1, English, had an instrumental role and was used for pragmatic and metalinguistic purposes (to make repairs, to save face, to ask questions and make comments, to provide an explanation, etc). More often than not, the L1 was activated in controlled, form-focused and acquisitionally driven switches. Nevertheless, when the learner had to overcome a lexical gap in order to keep the communicative flow, she often relied on her L2, German, as a default supplier of lexical information. This was particularly the case in unintentional language switches, or as the authors name them, switches without an identified pragmatic purpose that typically involved function words rather than content words.

The selection of an L2 as the default external supplier in L3 speech production depends on a number of factors, among which (psycho)typology, proficiency, recency, and the 'foreign language effect', also known in the literature as the 'L2 factor', defined as

(1) the tendency to avoid relying on the L1 in the belief that the mother tongue is inherently 'non-foreign', coupled with
(2) the tendency to favour non-native languages, which share a 'foreign language' status with the L3 (Williams & Hammarberg, 1998: 323).[2]

The authors suggest that the language that best meets these criteria is more likely to be selected as a supplier of lexical information. In their study, both English and German scored high in terms of typological proximity, proficiency and recency, and its L2 status seemed to tip the balance in favour of German.

We would like to close this overview with a note of caution regarding the validity of the criteria that can foster or inhibit the activation of a known language, be it the L1 or a L2. The above-mentioned factors interact in complex ways, their relative significance is hard to pin down, and there is a possibility that they could cancel each other out. Furthermore, the impact of the 'foreign language effect', which appears to be decisive in adult L3 acquisition, is bound to be of a lesser importance when two or more languages have been acquired in early childhood. Finally, it would be simplistic to think that one can set up a finite list of conditioning factors when so many circumstances beyond proficiency, proximity, recency and L2 status are known to impact the learning process in general and crosslinguistic associations in particular. Some of these factors depend less on linguistic issues (typology, proficiency and the like) than on cognitive features (different learning profiles, varying levels of metalinguistic awareness, degrees of attention and control in the realisation of the task, etc). Some are socio-psychological, such as the learner's motivation, attitudes and self-perception as a language learner and user. Others are the result of educational constraints, in relation to the learning environment and the learner's formal learning experience, the goals and the expectations set for teachers and learners in different academic traditions, the prevailing teaching methods and so on[3].

Multilingualism and metalinguistic awareness

Together with CLIN, metalinguistic awareness is a major subject of study in TLA research. Several leading publications have identified metalinguistic awareness as a key component of multilingual competence and as a factor that sets multilingual learners apart from monolingual learners, providing the former with a strategic advantage for further language learning (Gajo, 2001; Herdina & Jessner, 2002; Jessner, 2006; Moore, 2006a).

Needless to say, research on linguistic awareness did not begin with nor is restricted to multilingual studies and TLA research. The development of a capacity to view the first language as one linguistic system among others, to think about language in an abstract way and to manipulate linguistic data is a well-known outcome of bilingualism that has long been attested in the literature (for a critical review, see Baker, 2006). Moreover, metalinguistic awareness is consistently regarded as a *positive* outcome of the learning process, with beneficial effects in terms of the learner's cognitive development. For instance, Vygotsky wrote about the cognitive effects of learning a second language in the following terms:

> A child's understanding of his native language is enhanced by learning a foreign one. The child becomes more conscious and

deliberate in using words as tools of his thought and expressive means for his ideas. [...] The child's approach to language becomes more abstract and generalized. (Vygotsky 1986: 160)

In the field of SLA, the difference between 'knowing' and 'knowing about' a language has equally received considerable attention. As pointed out by Odlin (1989), Herdina and Jessner (2002) and Jessner (2006) among others, whatever the exact nature of the role that metalinguistic awareness plays, such awareness is a non-structural factor that interacts with crosslinguistic influences. The exact role of metalinguistic awareness in the learning process has generated substantial interest in the field of TLA. This is because the metalinguistic dimension introduces a level of conceptualisation that allows researchers to go beyond the strictly structural analysis of the interactions between known language systems (L1, L2, L3 ...) to take into consideration issues of perceived language distance, cognitive flexibility, linguistic creativity, control mechanisms, communicative sensitivity and so on. In all these areas, bilingual and multilingual learners consistently outperform monolingual learners, so much so that the learners' metalinguistic activity is now considered to be the locus for the emergence of a multilingual learning asset. By way of example, Gajo (1996) tested reading comprehension in Italian L3 by two groups of bilingual learners. Learners in the first group knew two Romance languages and learners in the second group spoke Romance and Germanic languages. The results did not vary significantly. This is interpreted as evidence that bilingual or multilingual learners exploit typological similarities when they are available but are equally able to resort to more general strategies to make sense of a written text (e.g. selective attention, knowledge of the world, contextual cues, intertextuality and analysis of topic markers).

Differences in theoretical and empirical perspectives notwithstanding, researchers pose the existence of a multilingual asset to conceptualise the enhanced language learning skills of multilingual learners: Gajo and Moore (*inter alia*) refer to an *atout plurilingue*, whereas Herdina and Jessner describe an *M-factor* or *multilingualism factor* in their dynamic model of multilingualism (Gajo, 2001; Herdina & Jessner, 2002; Jessner, 2006; Moore, 2006a, 2006b; Moore & Gajo, 2009).

Multilinguals are indeed credited with a higher strategic competence than monolinguals, which can be portrayed as a sophisticated toolbox for problem solving or, alternatively, as the ability to anticipate problems and to overcome linguistic, discursive or pragmatic shortcomings in order to successfully perform language learning tasks. In particular, it is widely believed that metalinguistic awareness enables learners to focus on structural similarities and differences or – if we follow the process approach devised by Bialystok – to analyse linguistic structures and selectively attend to those structures as a problem-solving strategy in the communicative task (Bialystok, 2001). Building on Bialystok's attention and control model, Herdina and Jessner (2002) argue that multilingual learners can rely on a particularly heightened monitoring mechanism. Not only does this mechanism fulfil the usual control functions in speech production (anticipating problems, correcting misunderstandings, using compensatory strategies to keep the communicative flow, etc), it also enables learners to draw on common resources in their linguistic repertoire and to keep their systems apart by checking for possible transfer phenomena.

The notion of metalinguistic awareness is particularly relevant from a classroom-centred perspective. Classroom interactions usually feature a high proportion of metalanguage, and it is an established fact that, in formal learning environments, metalinguistic uses of language (recasts, translations, explanations, autonymy[4]) are paramount. It is true that the importance given to metalinguistic tasks in the language-learning curriculum may vary according to different academic traditions. Nevertheless, the focus on form that results from metalinguistically oriented interaction is usually regarded as a necessary step in the acquisition process (Bange, 1992; Cicurel, 1985; Coste, 1985; De Pietro *et al.*, 1989; Sharwood Smith, 1981).

Research Purpose and Design

Research questions

Two research questions will be addressed in this chapter:

(1) What are the specific roles played by native and non-native languages in L3 learning? The literature of TLA is rich in publications that pose typological proximity as a condition for a second language to have a beneficial effect on the acquisition of a third one. In our study, the L1 (French) is typologically closer to the L3 (Spanish) than the L2 (English). We will investigate the relative influence of the factors that are known to favour reliance on a known language (proximity, proficiency, L2 status and so on) in this linguistic configuration.

(2) What is the impact of metalinguistic awareness in the learning process, both in connection with CLIN and as a learning asset?

Participants

For the present study, we have analysed the speech production of 42 non-specialist university students who were learning Spanish as part of their degree programmes at the Université de Technologie de Compiègne (UTC) in France. Each module consisted of 45 hours of teaching (three weekly hours) in one academic term. Eighteen participants in our survey were attending the module *Spanish for Beginners*, and the remaining 24 were enrolled in *Spanish III*, a module for higher intermediate learners who had already completed the courses *Spanish for Beginners* and *Spanish II* (for lower intermediate students) or who had already taken Spanish lessons at their high schools. For the overwhelming majority of these learners, exposure to Spanish was limited to the classroom. Of the 42 students, 40 identified French as their mother tongue. The remaining two students had Vietnamese and Arabic as their L1. Another three students had learnt French and another language simultaneously in early childhood (respectively, Hebrew, Wolof and Arabic). All other languages had been learnt in a formal setting, first at secondary school and then at university.

Table 3.1 summarises the learners' linguistic background and is based upon data provided by the learners themselves prior to the survey.[5] All 42 participants declared having good knowledge of English, the common denominator in their repertoires. Some of them were still studying English at the UTC. Sixteen participants (38%) had some knowledge of German, having learned the language at secondary school in France; two of the German-speaking students had also spent six months in Germany as exchange students/interns. One student was learning Italian and Spanish simultaneously.

Spanish was the L3 of 21 participants, typically, after French and English. Nineteen participants ranked it as their L4, usually after French, English and German, and the remaining two declared it was their L5. As already mentioned in the Introduction section, we use the label 'L3' for the sake of uniformity and economy, even if Spanish is not the third language in the learners' repertoire *stricto sensu*. We have not compared the performance of L3 versus L4 versus L5 learners. In our attempt to elucidate the role of known languages in L3 speech production, we have approached the analysis of the data based on the commonalities in the learners' linguistic profile, that is, French, their L1, and Spanish, the target language (be it their L3, L4 or L5), are Romance languages; all learners have knowledge of at least one Germanic language (English, their L2) and some know English and German.

Data

The corpus is made up of small group sessions that took place every 2 weeks as part of the Spanish modules taught at the language department at the UTC, along with three weekly hours of classes per academic term. These conversation sessions aimed to promote spontaneous, informal talk in Spanish in order to develop oral communication skills. They can be described as communication-oriented, with no explicit teaching of

Table 3.1 The participants' linguistic background

Participants	Proficiency in Spanish	L1	L2	L3	L4	L5
Ariel	Beginner	French	Hebrew	English	German	Spanish
Antoine	Beginner	French	English	German	Italian	Spanish
François	Beginner	French	English	German	Spanish	
Guillaume	Beginner	French	English	German	Spanish	
Agathe	Beginner	French	English	German	Spanish	
Caroline	Beginner	French	English	German	Spanish	
Pauline	Beginner	French	English	German	Spanish	
Camille	Beginner	French	English	German	Spanish	
Damien	Beginner	French	English	German	Spanish	
Liane	Beginner	French	English	German	Spanish	
Christophe	Beginner	French	English	German	Spanish	
Babacar	Beginner	French	Wolof	English	Spanish	
Saïd	Beginner	Arabic	French	English	Spanish	
Bin Minh	Beginner	Vietnamese	French	English	Spanish	
Laureen	Intermediate	French	English	German	Spanish	
Benoît	Intermediate	French	English	German	Spanish	
Maude	Intermediate	French	English	German	Spanish	
Christelle	Intermediate	French	English	German	Spanish	
Martin	Intermediate	French	English	German	Spanish	
Aziz	Intermediate	French	Arabic	English	Spanish	
Sarah	Intermediate	French	Arabic	English	Spanish	
Laurent	Beginner	French	English	Spanish		
Remy	Beginner	French	English	Spanish		
Christophe	Beginner	French	English	Spanish		
Bastien	Beginner	French	English	Spanish		
Florence	Intermediate	French	English	Spanish		

Crosslinguistic Interaction and Metalinguistic Awareness 35

Table 3.1 (*Continued*)

Participants	Proficiency in Spanish	L1	L2	L3	L4	L5
Alex	Intermediate	French	English	Spanish		
Guilhem	Intermediate	French	English	Spanish		
François	Intermediate	French	English	Spanish		
Pierre	Intermediate	French	English	Spanish		
Philippe	Intermediate	French	English	Spanish		
Céline	Intermediate	French	English	Spanish		
Léa	Intermediate	French	English	Spanish		
Emilie	Intermediate	French	English	Spanish		
Elodie	Intermediate	French	English	Spanish		
Eva	Intermediate	French	English	Spanish		
Vincent	Intermediate	French	English	Spanish		
Simon	Intermediate	French	English	Spanish		
Nicolas	Intermediate	French	English	Spanish		
Caroline	Intermediate	French	English	Spanish		
Caroline	Intermediate	French	English	Spanish		
Marc	Intermediate	French	Vietnamese	Spanish		

grammar and no written support. Each group was comprised of three or four students and a language tutor. Students were encouraged to make the most of their linguistic resources to keep the conversation going, and tutors generally restricted their participation to the minimum. Each session had a predefined topic, such as 'free time' for beginners or 'cinema' for intermediate learners, but learners were able to modify/expand on the topic or even suggest a change of topic. Topics can be said to provide a general framework for the discussion.

The data were collected between 2004 and 2006. We worked with a total of 12 groups, and we recorded 48 sessions, each of which lasted 30 minutes on average.

The empirical choice of working with relatively uncontrolled speech production in interactive settings was based on the hypothesis that the occurrence of language switches would be particularly high in less controlled tasks that require learners to go beyond their actual competence

Table 3.2 Analytical categories

Category	Function
1. PRAG	Manage the interaction, check mutual comprehension, open and close conversations, explain, repair, apologise ...
2. META	Reflect upon linguistic forms and functions. Comment on one's or somebody else's discourse, ask questions, request or offer assistance in order to solve difficulties in the comprehension or the production of speech.
3. INSERT	Explicit inserts: The inserted item occurs as part of a metalinguistic question or comment aimed to elicit or offer help. Implicit inserts: The insert is not framed by a metalinguistic comment or question but is discursively marked to signify a call for help, usually by means of rising intonation or other prosodic features. Non-elicit inserts: The insert is used to overcome gaps in the L3 without any explicit or implicit recognition by the speakers that they are producing a non-target item.

into unfamiliar territory and value communicative skills over formal correctness (Dewaele, 2001).[6] Also, the horizontal nature of learner-to-learner interaction (as opposed to the vertical relationship between teacher and learners in more formal classroom activities) creates favourable conditions for the observation of emergent, shared and situated multilingual strategies as learners collaborate to negotiate meaning in conversation (see Pica, 1994; Swain, 2000; and for the collaborative construction of meaning in multilingual communication, Bono & Melo-Pfeifer, 2008).

The data were analysed as follows:

(1) Language switches in L3 production were quantified and classified according to a functional typology of language switches (see Table 3.2).
(2) Metalinguistic sequences, that is, those stretches of conversation characterised by a shift of focus from content to form, were analysed qualitatively.

Typology of language switches

Language switches can consist of one or several words. They can be analysed formally, according to their position within an utterance (intrasentential switches), in-between utterances (extrasentential switches) or as a different utterance within a single turn (intersentential switches) (see Poplack, 1980, and, for a recent application to the analysis of trilingual conversation, Edwards & Dewaele, 2007). Most important, they serve different purposes in the conversation and can be used as a means to satisfy pragmatic, metalinguistic or linguistic needs. In order to investigate L1 and L2 role distribution in L3 learning, we have favoured a functional approach based on the typology devised by Williams and Hammarberg (1998) in their study of language switches in L3 speech production. Very briefly, Hammarberg and Williams identified four main categories:

(1) EDIT: switches with a pragmatic intent that enable the learner to 'edit' the conversation;
(2) META: metalinguistically driven switches; they convey questions or comments about the language;
(3) INSERT: lexical items that are mainly used to explicitly or implicitly call for help; this category also comprises non-elicit inserts, that is, lexical insertions that do not function as a request and
(4) WIPP ('without identified pragmatic purpose'): lexical items, usually function words, which do not seem to accomplish any specific pragmatic purpose in the conversation.

For the analysis of our data, we have treated NON-ELICIT INSERTS and WIPP inserts as belonging to the same category. In our view, both types of inserts share a fundamental characteristic: the speaker's underlying intention and, most importantly, her awareness that she has used a non-target word can be difficult to establish (see below). As we have argued in more detail elsewhere (Bono, 2008a), lexical inserts, regardless of whether they are content or function words, often help learners to overcome lexical gaps (in which case they can be classified as NON-ELICIT INSERTS) or accomplish pragmatic goals such as to remind other participants of their status as language learners, to express emotions or to negotiate aspects of the verbal interaction (in which case they fall within the category of pragmatic switches, EDIT).

Language switches in the speech of our L3 learners have been classified as follows:

(1) The first category, PRAG (EDIT in Williams and Hammarberg's typology), includes all **pragmatic switches**, that is, switches that express a pragmatic need or aim to create a certain illocutionary effect: to manage the conversation; to negotiate the task, the topic, participant status; to make repairs; to save face and so on. Typically, this category comprises discourse hedges, interjections, exclamations, brief requests and opening and closing turns.
(2) The second category, META, comprises **metalinguistic switches**, that is, language switches that enable the learner to make comments or questions about the target language. These comments or questions can refer to any aspect of the language: its syntax, its phonetic and

phonological features, its lexicon and so on. Vocabulary is the most frequent trigger of metalinguistic switches (e.g. *How do you say 'weather' in Spanish?*). A metalinguistic switch usually leads to the opening of a lateral sequence in the conversation and a shift of focus from content to form.

(3) The third category, INSERT, corresponds to **lexical insertions**, that is, L1 or L2 lexical units that are incorporated into the learners' speech production in L3. Following Williams and Hammarberg, three different types of inserts will be identified:

- EXPLICIT INSERT: They enable a participant to seek help from an interlocutor or, eventually, to offer help in the form of a translation or a recast. When the request is conveyed explicitly, the item occurs together with a metalinguistic question. In the above example, 'How do you say "weather" in Spanish?', *weather* is an explicit lexical insertion.
- IMPLICIT INSERT: A more economical way of requesting, or offering, help is by using a non-target lexical unit with specific prosodic and/or discourse markers. For example, a non-target word uttered after a pause and with rising intonation usually conveys an implicit request for help.
- NON-ELICIT INSERT: This subcategory includes lexical inserts that fit into the primary contents of the conversation but do not seem to function as a call for help. Discursively, they are not preceded or followed by a metalinguistic frame. From a pragmatic point of view, there seems to be no intention to elicit help, either directly or indirectly. And most importantly in some cases, learners appear to be unable to recognise the occurrence of a language switch (as evidenced by the absence of self- or other-initiated repairs in the conversation), so much so that it is difficult to assess whether the switch is intentional or not and whether a lexical insert is perceived, either by the speaker or by her interlocutors, to be a non-target item.

Results

This section is divided into four different parts. In the first two sections we present and discuss our findings regarding the number and nature of the 1371 language switches identified in the data with a view to analyse the functions accomplished by L1 and L2 in L3 speech production. The next section, *Language switches according to the learners' proficiency levels*, is devoted to the analysis of conversational sequences with underlying metalinguistic concerns, which may or may not contain a language switch but are motivated by crosslinguistic associations between known language systems.

Language switches in L3 speech production

We have been able to identify a total of 1371 language switches in conversations in Spanish L3. As shown in Figure 3.1, 18% of them ($n = 246$) accomplish a pragmatic function and 19% ($n = 265$) fall within the metalinguistic category. Inserts account for 63% of all switches ($n = 860$).

Figure 3.2 summarises the results for the three different types of lexical insertions:

The high frequency of implicit requests accomplished by means of a language switch can be attributed to the fact that IMPLICIT INSERTS afford an economic way of signalling a lexical gap. Participants clearly favour

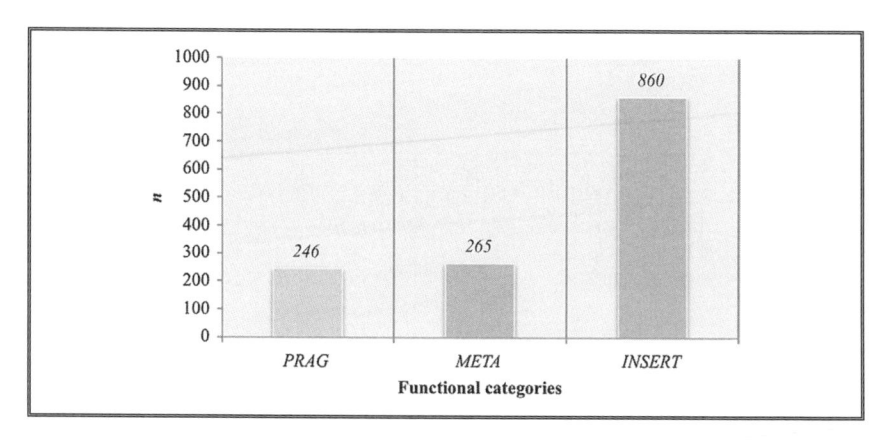

Figure 3.1 Language switches in L3 speech production

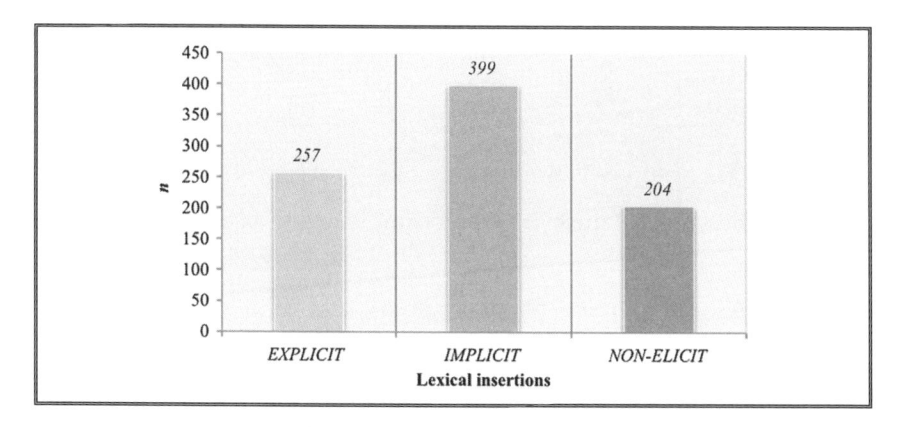

Figure 3.2 Different types of lexical insertions

lexical insertions over metalinguistic questions in order to elicit help from fellow participants, as illustrated by Example 1 here. A possible explanation for why learners prefer to seek assistance through lexical insertions is related to the nature of the task, which does not lend itself to lengthy metalinguistic explanations and the communicative pressure that participants face in order to keep the conversation going smoothly and with minimum interruption.

We have been able to identify 204 lexical insertions without elicitation. As already explained, these NON-ELICIT INSERTS differ from IMPLICIT INSERTS in that they do not feature discursive and prosodic markers that can be interpreted as a call for help. The learners do not pause nor raise their intonation, and the conversational outcome depends on other participants' reactions: in some cases, there will be a recast but in others, the insertion will go unnoticed, or at least, it will not be treated as a linguistic or communicative problem, as illustrated by the word *ten* in Example 2.

Example 1   *English translation*

LEARNER:	es una pequeña sala y la... l'ambiance?	It's a small venue and the... [SPA] the atmosphere? [FR]
TUTOR:	el ambiente	the atmosphere [SPA]
LEARNER:	el ambiente está muy buena pero...	There's a very good atmosphere but... [SPA]

Example 2   *English translation*

LEARNER A:	tengo una entrevista para una práctica esta tarde	I have an interview for an internship this afternoon [SPA]
LEARNER B:	¿dónde?	Where? [SPA]
LEARNER A:	en L'Oréal	at L'Oréal [SPA]
LEARNER B:	¿y te gusta esta práctica?	And would you like to do it? [SPA]
LEARNER A:	oh/no sé/hay ten chicas que quieren hacer esta entrevista en L'Oréal entonces ...	Oh/I don't know/there are [SPA] ten [EN] girls who want to do this interview with L'Oréal so... [SPA]

Language switches according to the learners'
proficiency levels

Figure 3.3 summarises the distribution of the language switches according to the learners' proficiency level in Spanish. As could be expected, beginners produce the higher number of switches, 61% of the total amount ($n = 843$), and intermediate learners produce the remaining 39% ($n = 528$).

The following are general observations about the type and number of switches per category per proficiency group:

PRAG. The frequency of pragmatic switches does not vary significantly from one group to the other. The switch consists of a word or, more frequently, of a short utterance that pursues an illocutionary aim. Typically, learners code-switch to apologise, to comply with politeness requirements or to manage conversational turns, for instance, if they inadvertently interrupt each other (Example 3). Language switches are equally frequent in the spontaneous expression of emotions, such as frustration in the face of insufficient knowledge of the language (*Je me suis lancé trop loin*, in Example 4).

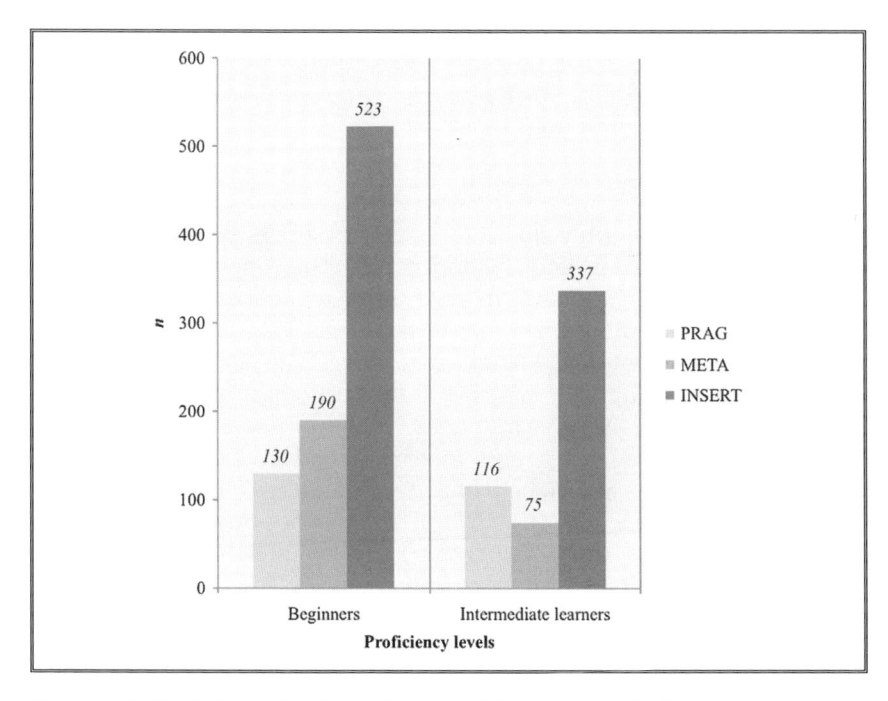

Figure 3.3 Proficiency levels and types of language switch

Example 3   *English translation*

| LEARNER A: | pardon! Vas-y | *Sorry! Go ahead [FR]* |
| LEARNER B: | toi d'abord | *You go first [FR]* |

Example 4   *English translation*

LEARNER:	no pueden ir en las familias y... son solo y no/mm ... no ... euh ... y son en compiègne solo en el samedi et dimanche?	*They can't go to their families and ... they are alone and they don't/ mm ... don't ... er ... and they are in Compiègne alone [SPA] on the Saturday and Sunday? [FR]*
TUTOR:	el fin de semana	*the weekend [SPA]*
LEARNER:	ah sí! Euh ... no puedo decir... no tengo vocabulario	*Oh yes! Er ... I can't say ... I don't have the vocabulary [SPA]*
TUTOR:	paciencia/paciencia	*Be patient [SPA]*
LEARNER:	je me suis lancé trop loin/trop loin	*I've overreached myself [FR]*

META. It is noteworthy that intermediate learners produce far fewer metalinguistic switches than beginners do. This does not necessarily mean that their conversations do not feature sequences with a focus on form; rather, being more proficient in the target language, they can ask questions or comment on the language (or languages) in Spanish (we will come back to metalinguistic switches in the Section *Source languages in the different types of language switches*).

INSERT. Both beginners and intermediate learners favour lexical insertions as a means to seek help or to overcome gaps in their vocabulary. Insertions account for 62% ($n = 523$) of all switches made by beginners, whereas they make up 64% ($n = 337$) of the switches produced by intermediate students. Insufficient knowledge of L3 vocabulary is the main trigger of lexical insertions.

Source languages in the different types of language switches

In terms of the languages activated in the language switches, 10.5% ($n = 144$) of the total number of switches involve a non-native language.

At first, this may appear a relatively low figure, but L3–L2 switches account for 63% of NON-ELICIT INSERTS, as we will see.

All switches in the PRAG and META categories involve French, the learners' L1. These results confirm previous findings in the literature indicating that in L3 speech production, the L1 accomplishes a mediating function or – in Williams and Hammarberg's terms – an instrumental role (Williams & Hammarberg, 1998). In our study, learners resort to French to achieve specific communicative or acquisitional aims beyond the mere expression of conversational content. Reliance on the L1 to accomplish such goals is encouraged by the fact that all participants in the survey share the same L1.

In the case of INSERTS, that is, non-target lexical borrowings in the production of speech in Spanish, results vary according to the type of insert. The L1, French, is clearly dominant in those cases in which the insertion is the result of an attempt by the learner to seek or to offer help by resorting to a non-target word. We have only identified a couple of L2 words in the categories EXPLICIT INSERT and IMPLICIT INSERT, and these are usually terms that do not have a French equivalent. Findings are significantly different when we look into lexical insertions without elicitation, which are not accompanied by discursive or prosodic markers of metalinguistic activity. As shown in Figure 3.4, L2 influence (or the combined influence of L1 and L2)[7] accounts for 63% of these lexical insertions. Non-native languages, and English in particular, supply lexical items that enable learners to overcome lexical gaps in communication-oriented switches.

In the following example, a learner resorts to the German *Monate* (*month*) and, there is nothing in his discourse to suggest that he is aware of having used a German word. When the tutor signals the need for a

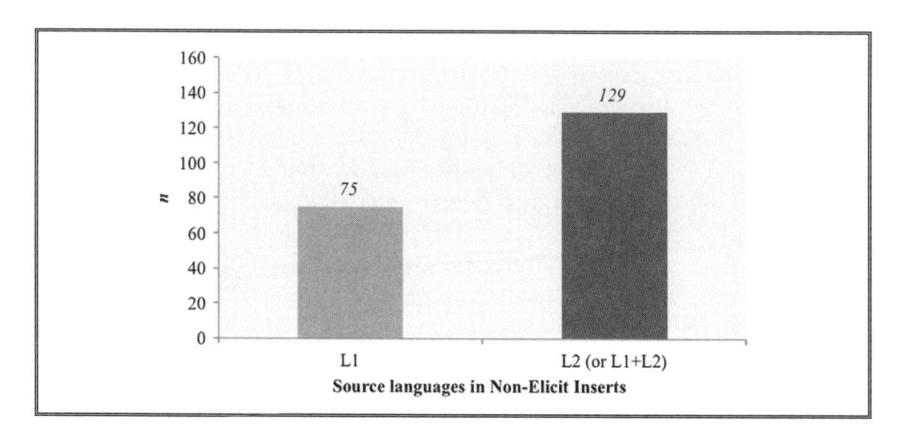

Figure 3.4 Source languages in non-elicit inserts

recast, this comes in the form of an intra-linguistic strategy, definition (*four weeks*):

Example 5   *English translation*

LEARNER:	tengo ... tengo pez/ tengo euh ...lo tengo después ella tiene ... un Monate	*I have ... I have fish/I have er ... I have it since she has ... a [SPA] month [GER]*
TUTOR:	¿un qué?	*a what? [SPA]*
LEARNER:	un ... cuatro semanas	*A ... four weeks [SPA]*
TUTOR:	ah! un mes	*Oh! a month [SPA]*
LEARNER:	un mes	*a month [SPA]*
TUTOR:	ah/lo tengo desde hace un mes/ok/y quién se ocupa de él cuando estás aquí? qui s'en occupe cuando estás en Compiègne?	*Oh/I've had it for a month/ok/and who looks after it when you are here? [SPA] who looks after it when you are in Compiègne [FR]?*
LEARNER:	mi padre	*my father [SPA]*

To further illustrate this point, the following L2 lexical inserts (all of them English borrowings) appear in our corpora without being discursively treated as such: *Muslim, German, picture, Chinese, end, can* (V), *difficult, long, my, two, so, than, but* and *yes*.

Discussion: The Foreign Language Effect

Why do French learners resort to English (and sometimes German) words when they interact in Spanish? On the basis of factors such as typological proximity, proficiency levels and frequency of use, French, the L1, should prevail. In other words, our learner in Example 5 above should have chosen the French word *mois* (EN: *month*) instead of its German equivalent. The learners' comparatively lower proficiency, the greater typological distance between Germanic languages and Spanish and the lower frequency of use of the former compared to French are all variables that seem to be neutralised by another factor that is specific to TLA, the **L2 factor** or **foreign language effect**. Both the L3 and the L2 share a 'foreign' status that sets them apart from the L1, which is perceived as inherently non-foreign. As our findings suggest, the different status of their linguistic systems is key to explain why learners favour reliance on their second languages as sources of linguistic information in the acquisition of yet another foreign language.

The possible association in the multilingual mind of words tagged as 'foreign' has already been attested in several publications (Hammarberg, 2001; De Angelis & Selinker, 2001; Selinker & Baumgartner-Cohen, 1995). According to De Angelis (2005), this cognitive association creates an identification problem, because learners fail to recognise that a word or expression does not belong to the L3 but to another non-native language (De Angelis, 2005; see also Clyne, 1997). It should be pointed out here that a majority of publications explore the hypothesis of a foreign language effect in association with L2–L3 typological proximity. Not only do our findings confirm the existence of a foreign language effect, this hypothesis is actually reinforced by the comparatively greater typological distance between L2 and L3 in our study.

The fact that the most commonly activated L2 is English calls for further analysis. English enjoys a special status in the linguistic and cultural repertoire of our learners, and this may reinforce the foreign language effect. For most of them, English is the foreign language *par excellence*, the language they choose first and they get to know better, the language whose command they all regard as compulsory (Bono, 2006, 2008a). English is the European lingua franca for all those students who embark on mobility programmes outside France and a language that exerts considerable influence through an array of cultural products with a young audience (music, film, the internet). Although an in-depth discussion of the role of English as an international language is not within the scope of this article, we would like to argue here that, when it comes to English, the possibility that *familiarity* may take precedence over *proximity* cannot be ruled out.

Another important question raised by our findings has to do with learners' awareness of L2–L3 interplay. Initially, non-elicit inserts appear to be unintentional. We acknowledge that it is extremely difficult to establish intentionality and levels of consciousness. Think-aloud protocols can help but, in our experience, learners are not always able to recognize crosslinguistic phenomena, let alone provide an elaborate explanation about them. From a discourse analysis perspective, there is nothing in the learners' speech production itself to suggest intentionality (no introductory question, no rising intonation, no self-repair, etc), and it is equally difficult to ascertain whether the other participants in the conversation identify the insert as such: even if they do realize that a non-target word has been used, they may choose to focus on that particular item (for example, to suggest an alternative word) or to ignore it. Pragmatic concerns – such as the desire to help someone save face by avoiding correcting a mistake – are too important here to be disregarded. In spite of these analytical problems, it is nevertheless important to point out that when a language switch does lead to a lateral sequence focused on linguistic form, this conversational activity opens up an invaluable opportunity for language acquisition (for further discussion on crosslinguistic comparison as a learning accelerator, see Bono, 2007).

Metalinguistic sequences in L3 speech production

So far, we have been able to establish that reliance on an L2 may help learners overcome a gap in their L3 interlanguage. In the light of these findings, it could be argued that L3 learners dispose of an additional source of lexical information when they attempt to use the L3 for communicative purposes and that multilingual learners can afford a larger reservoir of compensatory tools. However, if L3–L2 switches are (mainly) unintentional and L2–L3 interaction seems to result in non-target, deviant forms, how and to what extent can crosslinguistic interplay become a *learning asset*? This is where metalinguistic awareness enters the picture. Language switches are not the only way in which second languages are relevant for learning a third or additional language. As this section will attempt to demonstrate, L3 learners can also rely on their L2 to carry out a variety of analysis and monitoring tasks that require a great deal of attention and control and are fundamentally metalinguistic in nature.

In the Section *Language switches in L3 speech production*, we reported that, in our oral data, metalinguistic language switches always involve the learners' L1, French. However, the L2s cannot be dismissed as sources of metalinguistic activity. On the contrary, the cases in which systemic information from an L2 underlies a metalinguistic question or remark are very frequent in our corpora. This type of phenomenon cannot always be captured by an analysis of language switches like the one we have proposed so far. To accurately address them, we need to modify our analytical perspective to consider *what* is being said, regardless of the language the learners choose to say it. This change of perspective throws light on the fact that their conversations in Spanish are rich with metalinguistic (or formfocused) sequences in which learners deal with crosslinguistic issues involving one or several known languages in more or less explicit terms.

The occurrence of these sequences point toward a different kind of L2 influence, namely, the use of crosslinguistic comparison based on available L2 data. These sequences can target all aspects of the L3: phonetics, morphology, syntax, semantics and so on. Some involve a switch to the L1 (see Example 6, featuring a L3–L1 switch), and some do not involve a language switch at all. In the following exchange, not a single word of English is uttered, but the metalinguistic question (¿librería significa librairie o es como en inglés?) in which the learner tries to make sure that she is actually saying *bookshop* and not *library* is entirely due to her awareness that *librairie* in French and *library* in English mean different things:

Example 6 | *English translation*

LEARNER A:	qué haces en tu tiempo libre?	What do you do in your spare time? [SPA]
LEARNER B:	me encanta leer/quiero comprar el nuevo Harry Potter en inglés/mi prima tiene el libro en alemán pero ... no puedo leer Harry Potter en alemán porque no hablo so bien/**librería significa librairie o es como en inglés**?	I love reading/I want to buy the new Harry Potter in English/my cousin has the book in German but ... I can't read Harry Potter in German because I don't speak it [SPA] so [EN] well/ librería means [SPA] bookshop [FR] or is it like in English? [SPA]
TUTOR:	es como en francés	It's like in French [SPA]
LEARNER B:	mm/este fin de semana voy a paris/voy a una librería para comprar ... Harry Potter	mm/this weekend I go to Paris/I go to a bookshop to buy ... Harry Potter [SPA]

The following extract illustrates a semantic transfer by means of which learner A assumes that the adverb *actualmente* (*currently, nowadays*) has the same meaning as the English *actually* and is therefore different from the French *actuellement* (*currently, nowadays*). This creates a misunderstanding for the whole group and triggers a request for clarification, forcing the learner to be more explicit about his assumption:

Example 7 | *English translation*

LEARNER A:	escuchamos la grabación de las últimas palabras de salvador Allende	We listen to the recording of Salvador Allende's last words [SPA]
LEARNER B:	¿fue matado?	Was he killed? [SPA]
LEARNER A:	**actualmente se suicidó**	currently he committed suicide [SPA]
TUTOR:	quieres decir que en realidad se suicidó?	Do you mean he actually committed suicide? [SPA]
LEARNER A:	ah ça se dit pas 'actualmente'?	Oh you don't say [FR] 'currently'? [SPA]

| Tutor: | no/'actualmente' es 'ahora' | No/'currently' is 'now' [SPA] |
| Learner A: | ah/se suicidó... en realidad/en el Palacio de la Moneda | Oh/he... actually committed suicide/in the Palacio de la Moneda [SPA] |

Based upon the frequency of these metalinguistically driven sequences in the L3 learners' speech production, it seems possible to argue that known crosslinguistic differences between the L1 and one or several L2s creates the expectation of a difference in the L3.

Discussion: Multilinguals' Conscious Use of Crosslinguistic Comparison

Form-focused sequences similar to the ones we have presented in the previous section bear witness to multilingual learners' heightened capacity for analysing and monitoring their language as they speak. The analysis of L3 oral data suggests that in order to accurately identify the roles accomplished by second languages in TLA, we need to go beyond the study of language switches and investigate other forms of crosslinguistic activity based on the L2 data available to the learners and sustained by metalinguistic awareness.

As our findings suggest, metalinguistic sequences featuring a switch from the L3 to the L1 may well be motivated by an underlying, more or less implicit comparison involving other languages. From a communicative point of view, L3 learners engaged in verbal interaction use crosslinguistic comparison as a conscious strategy to anticipate or to solve problems. From an acquisitional point of view, ongoing crosslinguistic analysis combined with metalinguistic awareness has a high potential for language acquisition, if we assume that focus on form is a necessary step in this process.

The foreign language effect that we described in previous sections reduces the perceived distance between non-native languages. In light of our results, it may have an additional impact on TLA. The foreign language status of second or non-native languages may equally increase their visibility in the learning process, turning the L2 into a valuable source of information for hypothesis building and for alerting the learner of possible salient features in the L3.

Conclusion

In L3 speech production, metalinguistic exchanges (questions, remarks and their conversational follow-ups) featuring crosslinguistic associations between two or several known languages indicate that L2–L3 CLIN does not necessarily result in (often unintentional) lexical insertions whose communicative success may be relatively modest. On the contrary, L3 learners are sensitive to points of commonality between language systems and are able to exploit them to obtain a target language item and to attend to their production in deliberate and, in some cases, highly sophisticated ways.

The study of these learner strategies based on both crosslinguistic comparison and metalinguistic awareness raises considerable methodological challenges because of the varying degrees of verbalisation implied, ranging from very elaborate to non-existent. It may be relatively easy to identify a language switch, but it is quite difficult to pinpoint the actual source of learners' hypotheses about linguistic form and function if these hypotheses are informed by assumptions that do not leave recognisable traces in their discourse. However, absence of proof is not proof of absence, and working with conversational data can help to make up for this methodological difficulty. Verbal interactions provide a wealth of negotiation events in which problematic, deviant items can be dealt with by all the participants to ensure mutual comprehension and the accomplishment of their interactional goals.

To conclude, multilingual learners possess high levels of linguistic awareness, that is, an analytical approach to languages and the capacity to focus on their systematic features. These skills are mostly developed when acquiring non-native languages, and it is natural that multilingual learners refer to their second languages in the process of learning a third one. Our analysis of conversational data in Spanish as a third or additional language points towards reliance on English and, to a lesser extent, German, to obtain target language items. In the absence of metalinguistic awareness (i.e. of analysis and control), L2 influence may be perceived as hindering instead of favouring the learning process, hence the importance of encouraging learners to reflect upon the points of commonality and the differences between their languages to help them draw on common, shared resources in their repertoires.

Notes

1. 'Third language acquisition' (TLA) is used here as a terminological shortcut for 'third *or additional* language acquisition', a more satisfactory – albeit less economical – term. See De Angelis (2007: 11), Bono (2008a) and Hammarberg (2009) for further discussions on the use of the label 'L3' as a hyperonym and the epistemological and methodological issues raised by this choice.
2. Further theoretical insights into the 'L2 effect' or 'L2 factor' are to be found in Clyne (1997), De Angelis and Selinker (2001) and De Angelis (2005 *inter alia*).
3. For in-depth discussions of the socio-cultural and educational conditions that need to be met for multilingualism to be perceived as a learning asset in institutional contexts, see, for instance, Gajo (2001), Bono (2008a) and Moore and Gajo (2009).

4. Within the metalinguistic domain, 'autonymy' designates the special semantic case where a linguistic item refers to itself instead of referring to and describing objects in the mind or in the physical world (Authier-Revuz, 2003; Rey-Debove, 1978;). For example, in the utterance, '*enjoy* is a transitive verb', *enjoy* is used autonymically.
5. Caveats regarding self-reported proficiency levels apply.
6. Dewaele (2001) points out that the formality of the communicative situation crucially affects the choice of the language mode: formal situations tend to be monolingual, and informal conversations are characterised by a shift to mixed utterances.
7. In 26 of 129 language switches, the insert could be the result of the combined influence of two or more languages. Typically, the borrowed item is structurally similar in English and French – words such as *costume* (FR: *costume*) or *lesson* (FR: *leçon*) – and it is not possible, on the basis of pronunciation alone, to identify the source of borrowing.

References

Authier-Revuz, J. (2003) Avant-propos. In J. Authier-Revuz *et al.* (eds) *Parler des mots. Le fait autonymique en discours.* Paris: Presses de la Sorbonne Nouvelle.

Baker, C. (2006) *Foundations of Bilingual Education and Bilingualism.* Clevedon: Multilingual Matters.

Bange, P. (1992) À propos de la communication et de l'apprentissage en L2. *AILE* 1, 53–86.

Bialystok, E. (2001) *Bilingualism in Development. Language, Literacy, and Cognition.* Cambridge: Cambridge University Press.

Bono, M. (2006) La compétence plurilingue vue par les apprenants d'une L3: le plurilinguisme est-il toujours un atout? *Education et sociétés plurilingues* 20, 39–50.

Bono, M. (2007) La comparaison L2–L3, un tremplin vers l'acquisition trilingue. *Birkbeck Studies in Applied Linguistics* 2, 22–41.

Bono, M. (2008a) *Ressources plurilingues dans l'apprentissage d'une L3. Aspects linguistiques et perspectives didactiques.* Unpublished doctoral dissertation, Université Paris 3 – Sorbonne Nouvelle.

Bono, M. (2008b) Quand je parle en langue étrangère, je parle anglais. Conscience métalinguistique et influences interlinguistiques chez des apprenants plurilingues. In M. Candelier *et al.* (eds) *Conscience du plurilinguisme: pratiques, représentations et interventions* (pp. 93–108). Rennes: Presses Universitaires de Rennes.

Bono, M. and Melo-Pfeifer, S. (2008) Aspects contractuels dans la gestion des interactions plurilingues en contexte universitaire. *The Canadian Modern Language Review* 65 (2), 33–60.

Cenoz, J., Hufeisen, B. and Jessner, U. (eds) (2001) *Cross-linguistic Influence in Third Language Acquisition: Psycholinguistic Perspectives.* Clevedon: Multilingual Matters.

Cenoz, J., Hufeisen, B. and Jessner, U. (eds) (2003) *The Multilingual Lexicon.* Dordrecht: Kluwer Academic.

Cicurel, F. (1985) *Parole sur parole. Le métalangage en classe de langue.* Paris: Clé International.

Clyne, M. (1997) Some of the things trilinguals do. *International Journal of Bilingualism* 1/2, 95–116.

Clyne, M. (2003) *Dynamics of Language Contact*. Cambridge: Cambridge University Press.
Corder, S.P. (1981) *Error Analysis and Interlanguage*. Oxford: Oxford University Press.
Corder, S.P. (1983) A role for the mother tongue. In S. Gass and L. Selinker (eds) *Language Transfer in Language Learning* (pp. 85–97). Rowley, MA: Newbury.
Coste, D. (1985) Métalangages, activité métalinguistique et enseignement/apprentissage d'une langue étrangère. *DRLAV* 32, 63–92.
Coste, D. (2001) De plus d'une langue à d'autres encore. Penser les compétences plurilingues? In V. Castellotti (ed.) *D'une langue à d'autres, pratiques et représentations* (pp. 191–202). Rouen: Publications de l'Université de Rouen.
De Angelis, G. (2005) Multilingualism and non-native lexical transfer: An identification problem. *International Journal of Multilingualism* 2/1, 1–25.
De Angelis, G. (2007) *Third or Additional Language Acquisition*. Clevedon: Multilingual Matters.
De Angelis, G. and Dewaele, J-M. (2009) The development of psycholinguistic research on crosslinguistic influence. In L. Aronin and B. Hufeisen (eds) *The Exploration of Multilingualism* (pp. 63–77). Amsterdam: Benjamins.
De Angelis, G. and Selinker, L. (2001) Interlanguage transfer and competing linguistic systems in the multilingual mind. In J. Cenoz, B. Hufeisen and U. Jessner (eds) *Cross-linguistic Influence in Third Language Acquisition: Psycholinguistic Perspectives* (pp. 42–58). Clevedon: Multilingual Matters.
De Pietro, J-F., Matthey, M. and Py, B. (1989) Acquisition et contrat didactique: les séquences potentiellement acquisitionnelles dans la conversation exolingue. In E. Weil and H. Fugier (eds) *Actes du troisième colloque régional de linguistique* (pp. 99–124). Strasbourg: Université des Sciences Humaines et Université Louis Pasteur.
Dewaele, J-M. (1998) Lexical inventions: French interlanguage as L2 versus L3. *Applied Linguistics* 19 (4), 471–490.
Dewaele, J-M. (2001) Activation or inhibition? The interaction of L1, L2 and L3 on the language mode continuum. In J. Cenoz, B. Hufeisen and U. Jessner (eds) *Cross-linguistic Influence in Third Language Acquisition: Psycholinguistic Perspectives* (pp. 69–89). Clevedon: Multilingual Matters.
Edwards, M. and Dewaele, J-M. (2007) Trilingual conversations: A window into multicompetence. *International Journal of Bilingualism* 11 (2), 221–242.
Ellis, R. (1994) *The Study of Second Language Acquisition*. Oxford: Oxford University Press.
Gajo, L. (1996) Le bilingue romanophone face à une nouvelle langue romane: Un atout bilingue doublé d'un atout roman? *Études de Linguistique Appliquée* 104, 431–440.
Gajo, L. (2001) *Immersion, bilinguisme et interaction en classe*. Paris: Didier.
Gass, S. and Selinker, L. (eds) (1983) *Language Transfer in Language Learning*. Rowley, MA: Newbury.
Gass, S. and Selinker, L. (eds) (1994) *Language Transfer in Language Learning*. Amsterdam: John Benjamins.
Hammarberg, B. (2001) Roles of L1 and L2 in L3 production and acquisition. In J. Cenoz, B. Hufeisen and U. Jessner (eds) *Cross-linguistic Influence in Third Language Acquisition: Psycholinguistic Perspectives* (pp. 21–41). Clevedon: Multilingual Matters.
Hammarberg, B. (2006) Activation de L1 et L2 lors de la production orale en L3. Étude comparative de deux cas. *AILE* 24, 45–74.

Hammarberg, B. (2009) *Processes in Third Language Acquisition*. Edinburgh: Edinburgh University Press.
Hammarberg, B. and Williams, S. (1993) A study of third language acquisition. In B. Hammarberg (ed.) *Problem, Process, Product in Language Learning* (pp. 60–70). Stockholm, Sweden: Stockholm University.
Herdina, P. and Jessner, U. (2002) *A Dynamic Model of Multilingualism. Perspectives of Change in Psycholinguistics*. Clevedon: Multilingual Matters.
Hufeisen, B. and Lindemann, B. (eds) (1998) *Tertiärsprachen. Theorien, Modelle, Methoden*. Tübingen: Stauffenburg Verlag.
Jessner, U. (2006) *Linguistic Awareness in Multilinguals. English as a Third Language*. Edinburgh: Edinburgh University Press.
Kellerman, E. (1978) Giving learners a break: Native language intuitions as a source of predictions about transferability. *Working Papers on Bilingualism* 15, 59–92.
Kellerman, E. (1979) Transfer and non-transfer: Where are we now? *Studies in Second Language Acquisition* 2, 37–57.
Kellerman, E. (1983) Now you see it, now you don't. In S. Gass and L. Selinker (eds) *Language Transfer in Language Learning* (pp. 112–134). Rowley, MA: Newbury.
Kellerman, E. and Sharwood Smith, M. (eds) (1986) *Crosslinguistic Influence in Second Language Acquisition*. New York: Pergamon.
Moore, D. (2006a) *Plurilinguismes et École*. Paris: Didier.
Moore, D. (2006b) Plurilingualism and strategic competence in context. *The International Journal of Multilingualism* 3 (2), 125–138.
Moore, D. and Gajo, L. (inter alia) Introduction. French voices on plurilingualism and pluriculturalism: Theory, significance and perspectives. *International Journal of Multilingualism* 6 (2), 137–153.
Odlin, T. (1989) *Language Transfer. Crosslinguistic Influence in Language Learning*. Cambridge: Cambridge University Press.
Pica, T. (1994) Research on negotiation: What does it reveal about second-language learning conditions, processes and outcomes. *Language Learning* 44, 193–527.
Poplack, S. (1980) Somtimes I'll start a sentence in Spanish y termino en español: Toward a typology of code-switching. *Linguistics* 18, 581–618.
Rast, R. (2010) The use of prior linguistic knowledge in the early stages of L3 acquisition. *IRAL* 48 (2–3). Special issue.
Rast, R. and Trévisiol, P. (eds) (2006) L'acquisition d'une Langue 3. *AILE* 24.
Rey-Debove, J. (1978) *Le Métalangage*. Paris: Le Robert.
Ringbom, H. (2007) *Cross-linguistic Similarity in Foreign Language Learning*. Clevedon: Multilingual Matters.
Selinker, L. and Baumgartner-Cohen, B. (1995) Multiple language acquisition: "Damn it, why can't I keep these two languages apart?" *Language, Culture and Curriculum* 8, 115–121.
Sharwood Smith, M. (1981) Consciousness-raising and the second language learner. *Applied Linguistics* 11 (2), 159–168.
Swain, M. (2000) The output hypothesis and beyond. In J. Lantolf (ed.) *Sociocultural Theory and Second Language Learning* (pp. 97–114). Oxford: Oxford University Press.
Vygotsky, L. (1986; first Russian edition 1934) *Thought and Language*. Cambridge, MA: MIT Press.
Williams, S. and Hammarberg, B. (1998) Language switches in L3 production: Implications for a polyglot speaking model. *Applied Linguistics* 19 (3), 295–333.

Chapter 4
Transfer from L3 German to L2 English in the Domain of Tense/Aspect

ANNA S.C. CHEUNG, STEPHEN MATTHEWS and WAI LAN TSANG

Introduction

Language transfer is a central topic in the field of second-language acquisition (SLA) and third-language acquisition (TLA). The involvement of the additional third language in TLA complicates the picture with different possible sources and paths of transfer. Most studies to date have discussed transfer from an earlier acquired language to a learned one (forward transfer: e.g. Cenoz *et al.*, 2001). In comparison, little work has been done on the possibility of transfer in the reverse direction: from a later learned language to a previously acquired one (i.e. backward/reverse transfer from the third language, L3, to the second language, L2).

The purpose of the present study is to investigate the influence that L3 German may exert in proficient L2 English speakers with Chinese (Cantonese) as L1. Before presenting the study proper, a brief review of prior studies on backward transfer will be given, followed by a comparison of the three languages, English, German and Chinese (Cantonese) in terms of the perfect tense. Factors relevant to transfer including (perceived) language distance, recency and frequency will also be touched upon. After the review, the methodology of the study is examined. The performance of the participants in the two experimental tasks is presented and discussed in the results and discussion sections.

Background

Previous studies on backward transfer

In the course of SLA, the path of transfer can be in both forward and backward directions. Backward transfer from L2 to L1 has been studied mostly in the context of attrition (e.g. Seliger & Vago, 1991). Pavlenko and Jarvis (2002) have demonstrated the existence of backward transfer in postpuberty Russians who had been learning L2 English in the United States for three to eight years. They were asked to recite the content of two silent short films in Russian and English respectively. The findings revealed that some areas of morphosyntax, lexis and semantics were subject to bidirectional transfer, whereas other areas were influenced by L1, L2 or neither of the two languages.

The idea of bidirectional transfer can be extended to TLA in different directions and combinations. Two studies have examined backward transfer in the direction of L2 ← L3. Chuang (2002) discusses the issue of backward transfer in the context of L1 Chinese – L2 English – L3 German. The acquisition of English relative clauses by L1 Taiwan Chinese students learning L2 English and L3 German was investigated through grammaticality judgment, translation and sentence-combination tasks. The performance of the L3 German students (from two universities) was compared with those with only L2 English (from another university and a college). Results of this research showed that L3 German did not assist in the learning of L2 English, which was still subject to the L1 Chinese influence.

Contrary to Chuang, Griessler (2001) suggests that learning L3 French may improve learners' L2 English in terms of vocabulary and verb morphology. Grade 6 and 9 students from three Austrian high schools (an English immersion school, an L3 French school and an ordinary high school) participated in the study. They were asked to narrate a picture story in English. Results showed that the English immersion students performed best in lexical variety and accuracy of verb morphology, with the L3 French students coming second and the ordinary school students, last. Griessler concludes that L3 French helps improve L2 English in the domains studied. Although the language proficiency levels of the students in these two studies are not stated, and this may affect the reliability of the results, the two studies have pointed to the possibility of L3 influence on L2. Following this direction, the present study examines the possibility of backward transfer between two Germanic languages – L2 English and L3 German. Throughout this study, L3 refers to a third or additional language, following the definition of De Angelis (2007), since drastic differences between the acquisition of L3 and Ln had not yet been found, in contrast to those between L2 and L3 (Hammarberg, 2009).

The English present perfect and the German perfect

In English, the past simple tense indicates an event or action that happened before the time of speaking and is no longer related to the present moment, whereas the present perfect tense refers to an event or action that happened in the past but is still connected to the present (Huddleston & Pullum, 2002: 142–143). The difference between the two tenses, according to Comrie (1985: 25), lies in the aspect of 'current relevance', which can only be implied by the present perfect tense. Because of present relevance, past time adverbs, such as *last year* or *three months ago*, are incompatible with the present perfect tense (Huddleston & Pullum,

2002: 143). However, the division between the corresponding tenses is not that clear in German. Both Präteritum (*preterite*) and Perfekt (*perfect*) tenses can refer to a past action or event, and they can also depict a past action or event that has present relevance (Durrell, 2002: 296–299).

Sentences (1) to (4) illustrate the differences between English and German in presenting a past situation denoted by the past time adverb *yesterday*. To describe the action of writing a letter the day before in English, the verb *write* has to appear in the past simple form *wrote*, as in (1). The use of the present perfect tense, as in (2), is ungrammatical. In German, however, the verb *schreiben* (*write*) can appear in either the preterite form *schrieb* (*wrote*), as in (3), or the perfect form *habe + geschreiben* (*have + written*), as in (4).

(1) I wrote a letter yesterday.
(2) *I have written a letter yesterday.
(3) Gestern   schrieb   ich   einen   Brief.
    yesterday write-1SG-PST   1SG   ART-INDF.M-ACC   letter
    'I wrote a letter yesterday.'
(4) Gestern   habe   ich   einen   Brief   geschrieben.
    yesterday have-1SG-PRS   1SG   ART-INDF.M-ACC   letter   write-PRF
    'I wrote a letter yesterday.'

In English, the present perfect tense is formed by a combination of the auxiliary verb *have* and the past participle form of a verb, as in (5). The German perfect has a similar structure but has an option of two auxiliary verbs: *haben* (*to have*) or *sein* (*to be*) (i.e. *haben/sein* + Partizip Perfekt [*past participle*] form of the verb), as in (6) and (7). The choice of auxiliary verb depends on the main verb, and the auxiliary conjugates depending on the subject.

(5) I have baked a cake.
(6) Ich   habe   einen   Kuchen   gebacken.
    1SG   have-1SG-PRS   ART-INDF.M-ACC   cake   bake-PRF
    'I have baked a cake./I baked a cake.'
(7) Er   ist   nach   Deutschland   gefahren.
    3SG   be-3SG-PRS   to   Germany   go-PRF
    'I have been to Germany./I went to Germany.'

The Cantonese experiential aspect marker *gwo3*

In this study, Cantonese and Mandarin are grouped under the umbrella term 'Chinese' in light of the structural similarities between the two languages in terms of the target structures concerned, that is, the verbal aspect system and the equivalents of the present perfect. Cantonese, in contrast with English and German, does not use tense but aspect markers to refer to the nature of events and activities (e.g. perfective vs. imperfective). Among these markers, *gwo3* is used to indicate a sense of completion or experience as implied by the present perfect tense, as in (8), but may also be used for events without current relevance, as in (9) (Matthews & Yip, 1994: 206–208).

(8) ngo5   tai2 gwo3   nei1   bun2   syu1
    1SG   look-PFV   this   CL   book
    'I have read this book.'
(9) keoi5   cam4 jat6   gin3 gwo3   nei1   go3   jan4
    3SG   yesterday   see-PFV   this   CL   person
    'S/he saw that person yesterday.'

Factors underlying transfer

The factors affecting transfer are discussed in detail in works on SLA (e.g. Ellis, 1994, 2008; Odlin, 1989). Essentially the same factors are applicable in TLA (e.g. De Angelis, 2007; Jarvis & Pavlenko, 2008). Among these factors, (perceived) language distance, recency and frequency are most relevant to the present study.

Language distance refers to the typological and/or genetic distance between two languages while perceived language distance refers to the learner's judgment, which may be different from the actual distance (Kellerman, 1977). A number of studies show that transfer is more likely to occur between closely related languages than distant languages (e.g. Ahukanna *et al.*, 1981; Bouvy, 2000; De Angelis & Selinker, 2001).

Recency refers to the effect of the most recently used and/or acquired language on the target language. Dewaele's (1998) study shows that the most recently learned or used language – the 'active' language – is the source of lexical transfer in the L3 French production of L2 English learners. However, there are still controversies over the recency effect, with some studies showing influence from less recently used languages (see De Angelis, 2007, for discussion).

Frequency, as noted by Jarvis and Pavlenko (2008), may also influence the use of a structure in the target language. Selinker (1969, 1983) observes that the higher the frequency of a certain structure in L1 is, the higher the chance that a similar structure would appear in the learner's L2. Andersen (1983) further extends this factor/notion to include similar structures in L2.

Research Hypothesis

Because of the overlap between English and German in terms of past simple and present perfect tenses, it is hypothesized that, in the case of L1 Chinese (Cantonese), L2 English and L3 German, L3 German may

Transfer from L3 German to L2 English

have a negative influence in the acquisition of the present perfect–past simple contrast in L2 English (Table 4.1).[1]

The hypothesis is operationalized as follows:

L2 English learners with German as an L3 will be more likely to use the English present perfect tense to refer to the past than controls without knowledge of German.

The mapping of tense/aspect forms to past situations and the predicted mappings in the learners' English are shown in Figure 4.1.

Table 4.1 A comparison of the corresponding tense used in (a) past situations and (b) past situations with present relevance in standard English, German and L2 English of L3 German learners

	Corresponding tenses		
			Prediction
Actions/Events	English (L1)	German (L1)	English (L2) of L3 German learners
Past	Past simple	Preterite/perfect	Past simple/present perfect
Past with present relevance	Present perfect	Preterite/perfect	N/A

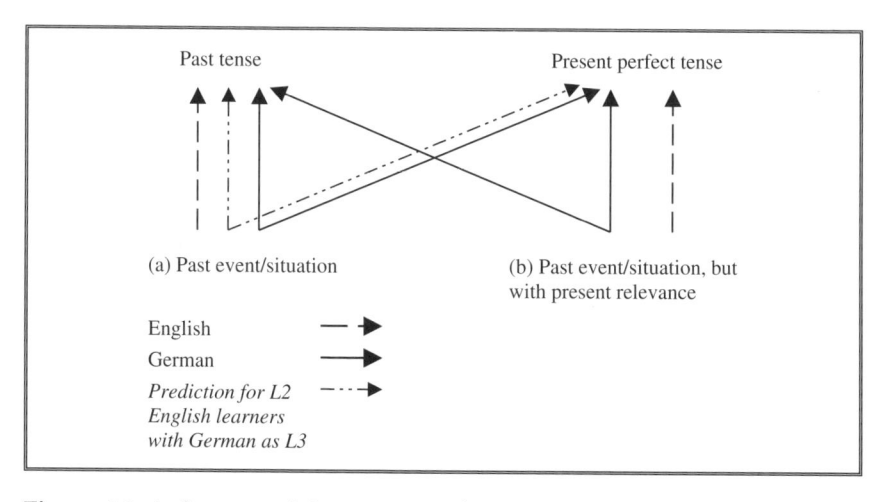

Figure 4.1 A diagram of the corresponding tense used in (a) past situations and (b) past situations with present relevance in standard English, German and L2 English of L3 German learners

Methodology

To test the hypothesis, a writing task and an acceptability judgment task were used.

Tasks

The English writing task was carried out between January and June 2009. The aim of this task was to identify the choice of tenses in recalling a past situation that might exhibit L3 German influence. Prior to this task, the experimental group participants (i.e. L3 German students) were asked to hand in their take-home writing assignment on the topic 'An embarrassing situation' or 'My time in Europe: My nice and my embarrassing experience'. (The slight difference in the topic arose because the L3 German participants were recruited from two German classes taught by different teachers.) This topic was chosen for the present research because it required the students to recount past events in their writing. The German essays were completed five to six months prior to the English writing task. The students were asked to produce an English composition with essentially the same content in the presence of the researcher. The essay produced in the writing task was not a mere translation of the German one because they were not allowed to refer to their German essay during the task. The participants were, however, allowed to go through their German essay before writing the English essay if they informed the researcher that they had forgotten the content. The control group participants were asked to write an English essay on the topic 'An embarrassing situation'.

The judgment task was conducted between April and June 2009. The experimental and the control group participants were asked to rate 26 English sentences on a four-point Likert scale (with 1 meaning 'not acceptable' and 4 meaning 'acceptable'). The composition of the task items was as follows:

- Five ungrammatical present perfect items
- Five grammatical past tense items
- Five sentences with ungrammatical agreement
- Five sentences with grammatical agreement
- Six distractors

There was an even split between grammatical and ungrammatical sentences. Each ungrammatical sentence contained only one error (see Appendix A for the full list of sentences). The test items were randomly ordered into three versions that were given at random to the participants so as to minimize extralinguistic factors such as ordering effects (e.g. Birdsong, 1989). The aim of the judgment task was to assess the acceptability of (nontarget uses of) the present perfect tense, the past simple tense and subject–verb agreement. Only the results for the present perfect category are reported here.

Participants

Two groups of participants were recruited: an experimental group and a control group. All were undergraduates from an English-medium university in Hong Kong. The experimental group consisted of intermediate L3 learners of German enrolled in a third-year level course, who have Chinese (Cantonese) as their L1 and English as their L2. The control group consisted of L2 English learners without knowledge of European languages other than English. Thus, the participants of this group could take languages like Japanese, Korean or Thai as their third language.[2] Three students (one from the experimental group and two from the control group) stated that English was the L3 with the L2 being Mandarin. Since Mandarin and Cantonese are regarded as Chinese in this study, these L3 English cases were also counted as L2 English. One student also indicated that both Mandarin and German were L3. Students in the experimental group were in Years 3 and 4 of their undergraduate studies, whereas those in the control group were in Years 2 and 3.

A total of 23 participants completed the narrative writing study, with 12 from the experimental group and 11 from the control group. Twenty-one of them also participated in the judgment task.[3] Altogether, 37 students participated in the judgment task, with 26 from the experimental group and 11 from the control group.

The participants were asked to complete a questionnaire about their language background in order to understand more about their language repertoire. The total number of languages spoken/being learned by the two groups is displayed in Table 4.2 and Table 4.3.

Data analysis

Writing task

The verb phrases in the essays were analyzed in light of the focus of the study and the coding system, as shown in Table 4.4.

Codes T1 to T4 refer to the nontarget use of different tenses for past situations. T1 means that the participant used the present perfect tense for a past situation. T2 refers to cases where the present perfect progressive form was used for a past situation. T3 indicates that the present simple tense was used for a past situation. T4 denotes the use of past perfect tense for a past situation. In this study, focus was put on T1 and T2 since these two were related to the hypothesis that present perfect tense would be used in a past situation, whereas T3 and T4 were used for the investigation of possible L1 Chinese influence. The definition of *nontarget* is a tense (e.g. present perfect, present perfect progressive and present simple) used in a context where the past simple is expected in native English. Any combination of the auxiliary verb *have* and a verb (even though it might not be the past participle or might be spelled

60   New Trends in Crosslinguistic Influence and Multilingualism Research

Table 4.2 Languages spoken/being learned by the experimental group

Languages	Number of participants	
	Task 1 – Writing task	Task 2 – Judgment task
Cantonese	12	26
English	12	26
Mandarin	12	26
German	12	26
Danish	0	1
Italian	1	1
French	1	1
Spanish	1	1
Korean	1	2
Japanese	2	2

Table 4.3 Languages spoken/being learned by the control group

Languages	Number of participants	
	Task 1 – Writing task	Task 2 – Judgment task
Cantonese	11	11
English	11	11
Mandarin	11	11
Korean	1	1
Japanese	4	4
Thai	1	1
French	1	1

incorrectly) was counted as an instance of nontarget use of the present perfect, as in (10).

(10) Moreover, I **have knew** many friends.

Occurrences of the same verb in different past situations showing the same nontarget use were counted as many times as they appeared in the essays.

Table 4.4 Codes and their meaning with examples

Codes	Meaning	Examples of nontarget use
T1	Present perfect tense for past	Last summer, I **have been** to Bremen in Germany for a German summer course.
T2	Present perfect progressive tense for past (progressive)	I **have been living** in a host family, whereas there is an old woman living alone with two cats.
T3	Present simple tense for past	One man came to me and said, 'I **can** hear you even I was shopping in the shop!'
T4	Past perfect for past	As I was almost late to school, I **had rushed** to school and therefore looked even more embarrassing.

Judgment task

The five sentences that contained nontarget uses of the present perfect tense in the judgment task were analyzed in this study:

(11) *John **has traveled** to a number of European countries during the summer of 2007.
(12) *Yesterday, I **have celebrated** my friend's birthday with his parents.
(13) *My brother **has paid** a 100-dollar fine for his overdue books last week.
(14) *Last Christmas, I **have received** a pair of boots as a Christmas present.
(15) *While they were walking their dog this morning, they **have witnessed** a car accident.

The rating given by each participant on each sentence was recorded and analyzed using SPSS.[4] A higher rating given to a sentence would mean that the participant was more likely to accept it as a grammatical sentence.

Results

Writing task

Of the 12 English essays written by the L3 German learners, four contained nontarget uses of the present perfect tenses, amounting to a total of 16 instances (Table 4.5). The control group did not show any such nontarget uses in their essays (Table 4.6).

Table 4.7 shows representative samples containing the nontarget use of the present perfect found in the English narratives of the four L3 German learners.

Table 4.5 Nontarget use in relation to past situations found in the English writing task by the experimental group

Participants	Frequency of nontarget use of a tense			
	Present perfect	Present perfect progressive	Total	Total no. of verbs denoting past situations
G3	3	1	4	34
G5	4	0	4	27
G7	1	0	1	52
G12	7	0	7	14
Others	0	0	0	233
Total	15	1	16	360

Table 4.6 Nontarget use in relation to past situations found in the English writing task by the control group

Participants	Frequency of nontarget use of a tense			
	Present perfect	Present perfect progressive	Total	Total no. of verbs denoting past situations
Total	0	0	0	211

Two common characteristics were found among the four L3 German learners:

(i) They used both past simple and present perfect tenses in their English narratives, and
(ii) all the verbs that were found with nontarget use of the English present perfect tense take the auxiliary verb *haben* (*to have*) in German, except for *gegangen* (*have gone*) (Table 4.8).

Table 4.8 compares the nontarget usage of the English present perfect tense and the corresponding forms of the German perfect tense. The verbs chosen were those found in the 16 nontarget uses of the four L3 German students.

Judgment task

The distribution of the four-point scale ratings as indicated by the two groups is shown in Figure 4.2. In general, more control group

Table 4.7 Sample English sentences containing nontarget use of present perfect by the L3 German learners (G3, G5, G7 and G12)

Participants	Sentences containing nontarget use of English present perfect tense
G3	Last summer, I **have been** to Bremen in Germany for a German summer course.
G5	During my time in Europe, I **have spent** a month in Germany.
G7	**I've had** enough, and I was suffering so badly that I need a toilet immediately.
G12	After the course, I **have been** to three German cities: Nuremberg, Munich and Frankfurt.

Table 4.8 Nontarget use of English present perfect and their German equivalents

English present perfect	German perfect
have been (in the context of the respective essays) = have gone; have gone	gefahren (sein/haben); gegangen (sein)
have lived (originally have been living)	gelebt (haben)
have finished	beendet (haben)
have waited (originally have kept waiting)	gewartet (haben)
have spent	verbracht (haben)
have visited	besucht (haben)
have encountered	gestoßen (sein/haben)
have had	gehabt (haben)
have seen	gesehen (haben)
have learned	gelernt (haben)
have known (originally misspelled)	kennengelernt (haben)
have bought	gekauft (haben)

Percentage of ungrammatical English present perfect items

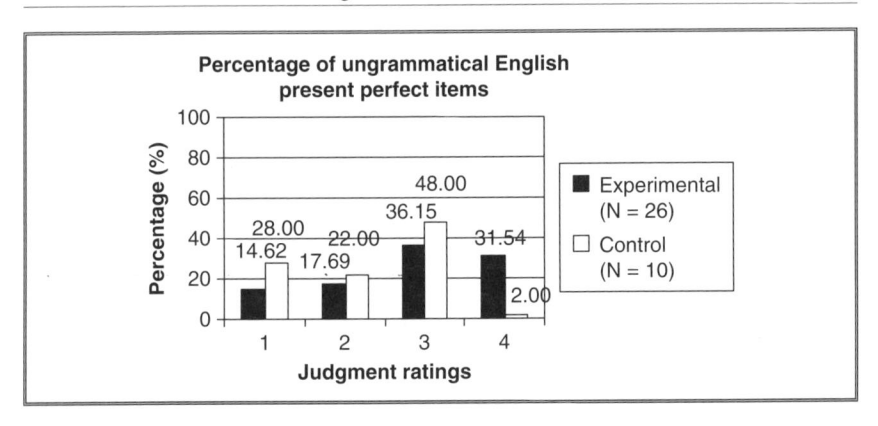

[Bar chart showing Judgment ratings 1–4 with Experimental (N = 26) and Control (N = 10) groups:
- Rating 1: Experimental 14.62, Control 28.00
- Rating 2: Experimental 17.69, Control 22.00
- Rating 3: Experimental 48.00, Control 36.15
- Rating 4: Experimental 31.54, Control 2.00]

Figure 4.2 Distribution of the responses of ungrammatical English present perfect tense items given by the experimental and control groups

participants tended to reject (i.e. by choosing '1' and '2') the ungrammatical English present perfect items than those of the experimental group (50% vs. 32.31%). A more detailed investigation shows that the percentage of controls who rejected the test sentences with a rating of '1' was nearly twice that of the experimental group (28% vs. 14.62%). In contrast, the number of experimental participants accepting the ungrammatical sentences with a rating of '4' was nearly 16 times that of the control group (31.54% vs. 2.00%). An independent-samples t-test shows that there was a significant difference between the two groups in choosing the rating of '4', with the percentage of experimental participants ($M = 1.58$, $SD = 1.47$) treating the ungrammatical present perfect items as grammatical being higher than the controls ($M = 0.10$, $SD = 0.32$); $t\ (30.14) = 4.83$, $p < 0.05$).

The mean rating of each group was calculated by the average of the total ratings of the five sentences given by each participant. Figure 4.3 shows the mean ratings on the scale from '1' to '4' of the judgment sentences containing nontarget use of the English present perfect tense. An independent-samples t-test was used to compare the two groups. Results show that the mean of the judgment ratings given by the experimental group ($M = 2.85$, $SD = 0.71$) was significantly higher than that of the control group ($M = 2.24$, $SD = 0.74$); $t\ (34) = 2.28$, $p < 0.05$).

Discussion

The results provide strong evidence for an influence of L3 German on L2 English in the domain studied. In the writing task, 16 cases of nontarget use of the present perfect tense were found in the experimental group versus zero cases in the control group. In the judgment task, the

Judgment task

- Ratings of ungrammatical English present perfect items: Experimental (N = 26) = 2.85; Control (N = 10) = 2.24

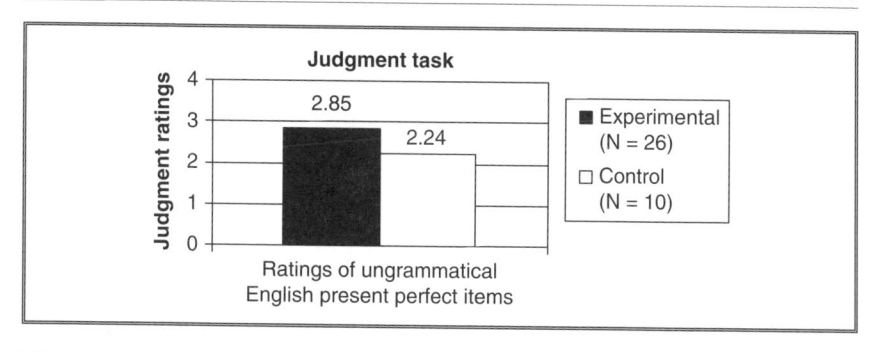

Figure 4.3 Mean ratings of ungrammatical English present perfect items given by the experimental and control groups

mean ratings given by the L3 German group to the nontarget English present perfect items were significantly higher than those for the control group.

Nontarget use of English present perfect tense in the narrative task

From the data collected in the writing task, 4 out of 12 L3 German learners were found to produce nontarget uses of the present perfect tense in their English (G3, G5, G7 and G12). The tendency for G7 to produce nontarget English present perfect patterns seems to be weak since there was only one instance out of 52 past situations. However, it is evident that the other three L3 German learners (i.e. G3, G5 and G12) had internalized the use of the English present perfect tense as applicable to past situations without current relevance. Their nontarget use of the present perfect tense can be viewed as systematic to varying degrees.

G12 was the most systematic user of the present perfect, using this tense to refer to past situations in 7 out of 14 instances. It appears that this participant has a tendency to substitute the present perfect tense for the past simple tense and, therefore, can be argued to have internalized the equivalence between the English present perfect and the German perfect. This claim is further supported by the complete absence of the German preterite in the German narrative, in which only the German present and perfect tenses were used.

G3 also seemed to have internalized the equivalence of German preterite and perfect tenses in describing past situations in English, as evidenced by three observations. First, the juxtaposition of both the present perfect and past tenses in the same sentence linked with the conjunction *but* and sharing the same past time reference, as shown in (16), suggested that the two tenses were treated as *interchangeable* by this learner.

(16) I **have kept** waiting outside for nearly half an hour but I was unable to seek help.

Second, the present perfect *have* in (17) was used as an afterthought (*have* was inserted with an arrow in the original script), resulting in an error, which is an indication that the present perfect tense was regarded as *more grammatical* than the past simple tense.

have
(17) One day when I ∧ **finished** school stuff and went back to the host, I saw one of those cats lying on the stairs in the front gate.

Third, the present perfect progressive in (18) was used to refer to a past event, suggesting that the present perfect (progressive in this case) was *a counterpart* of the past progressive tense (i.e. *was living*) in this learner's mind.

(18) I **have been living** in a host family whereas there is an old woman living alone with two cats.

It seems that G5 also treated the English present perfect and past simple tenses as equivalent. The English present perfect and past tenses were found in constructions with the same temporal preposition phrase introduced by *during*, as in (19) and (20).

(19) During my time in Europe I **have spent** a month in Germany.

(20) During my time in Europe, I also **had** bad experience.

Two other examples support this claim about G5. On the surface, (21) and (22) are ambiguous because they can be explained in two ways: they can be either (a) a mixture of present perfect and past tenses in the same sentence or (b) an indication that the auxiliary verb *have* was omitted for the second half of the sentence because of the presence of the conjunction *and*. Between these two explanations, the intention of the writer in (22) appeared to be the latter, as indicated by the German version presented in (23). In this sense, (22) and (23) are a matching case in which the omission of the perfect auxiliary in the second conjunct is applied to both languages. This suggests that (21) and (22) can be interpreted as coordinate sentences with the perfect auxiliary *have* applying to both verbs.[5]

(21) Although I **have encountered** some difficulties and **had** some bad experience during my travel, I still think that my time in Europe was good.

(22) It is because I **have seen** many beautiful landscape and **learnt** a lot.

(23) Ich **habe** viele   fantastische Landschaften **gesehen** und viel   **gelernt**.
     I   have many   fantastic   landscapes   seen   and many   learned

As most of the English verbs shown in Table 4.8 take the German auxiliary verb *haben* (*to have*), the L3 German students may have associated the verbs with their corresponding forms in German perfect (i.e. *haben* + verb) when they were expressing a similar meaning in L2 English.

Judgment of ungrammatical items

The average ratings of the nontarget English present perfect sentences of both groups also support the claim that the L3 German learners' perception of the English present perfect tense was somewhat different from that of the control group. The rating of the experimental group ($M = 2.85$) was nearer to the rating of '3' on the scale from '1' to '4', whereas the control group ($M = 2.24$) was closer to the rating of '2', and the difference was statistically significant. In other words, the L3 German learners were more likely to accept the nontarget use of the English present perfect tense than those without the knowledge of a European L3.

Regarding the percentage of learners accepting the English ungrammatical present perfect sentences, the experimental group was more likely to accept ungrammatical English present perfect sentences than the control group. They even had a significantly higher tendency to judge them as grammatical with a rating of '4', outnumbering the control group by nearly 16 times (31.50% vs. 2.00%). From another perspective, the experimental group was less inclined to reject these ungrammatical sentences with a rating of '1' than the controls (14.60% vs. 28.00%). These results reveal that the German L3 learners tended to treat the English present perfect tense as equal to the German perfect, which is very likely to be because of the result of the overlap between the structure of the German perfect and English present perfect tenses and also the equivalence between German preterite and perfect. This result confirms the prediction that German L3 learners tend to refer to past situations with the English present perfect tense.

Matching between English and German versions

A comparison between the English and the German versions of the compositions of those learners who made the error systematically (at least three times) also revealed their tendency to extend the coverage of the German perfect tense into English. Table 4.9 displays some representative examples of the matching and mismatching cases. A matching case means there is a match between the tense and aspect form in both the English and the German narratives (i.e. both versions use the perfect form in describing the same situation).

Table 4.10 shows the matching rate between the English and German versions, which is quite impressive (8 matches out of 16) when compared with that of the mismatches (3 pairs out of 16).

To summarize, the German narratives showed a match with the students' English tense usage in as many as 8 out of 16 cases.

Table 4.9 Examples of matches and mismatches between nontarget use of present perfect found in the English and German narratives

Participants	Languages	Sentences containing English present perfect error(s)	Matching tense/ aspect form?
G3	English	Last summer, I **have been** to Bremen in Germany for a German Summer Course.	No
	German	In diesem Sommer **fuhr** ich nach Europa. *(Similar meaning)*	
G5	English	It is because I **have seen** many beautiful landscape and learnt a lot.	Yes
	German	Ich **habe** viele fantastische Landschaften **gesehen** und viel gelernt.	
G12	English	Moreover, I **have knew** many friends.	Yes
	German	Ich **habe** viele Freunden **kennengelernt**.	
G12	English	I **have bought** many things in Europe especially chocolate.	Yes
	German	In Europa **habe** ich viele **gekauft**, zum Beispiel, Kleidung, Spielzeug, Rotwein, und so weiter.	

Table 4.10 Matches between nontarget use of present perfect found in the English narratives and the equivalent (or of similar meaning) found in the German narratives

Matches	Mismatches	Unclear	No corresponding structure	Total
8	3	1	4	16

Factors underlying the influence of L3 German on L2 English

The above analysis of the 16 cases of nontarget use of the English present perfect tense and the eight matching cases in the same learners' German narrative lends support to the hypothesis that L2 English learners with L3 German are more likely to use the English present perfect tense to refer to the past than those who do not have knowledge of German. The judgment data support this tendency, which corresponds to the questionnaire data as well. When the L3 German learners were asked to indicate how their English was influenced by German on a scale with the options 'always', 'usually', 'often', 'sometimes', 'seldom' and 'never', the largest number of learners chose 'sometimes'.[6] These findings can be further interpreted in terms of actual and perceived language distance between English and German, recency of use and/or acquisition and frequency of use of a structure in a language.

The actual language distance between English and German is very close since they are typologically similar when compared to Chinese, as well as being genetically related. In terms of the present perfect and past simple tenses, these two languages look even more similar, with overlapping functions and structures. As reviewed by De Angelis (2007), learners of a language are more likely to be influenced by a typologically closer language, whether it is their L1 or not. To some L3 German learners (like the ones in the study), the similarity between these two tense structures seems to be extended and applied to their English mental grammar, thereby influencing their choice of using the English present perfect tense in expressing past situations. When the L3 German learners were asked in a questionnaire about their views on the difference between Chinese–English, English–German and Chinese–German in terms of grammar, they indicated that English–German were relatively closer to each other when compared to that of the other two combinations (Figure 4.4). Such views are consistent with an explanation in terms of perceived similarity or perceived language distance.

Recency of use (e.g. Dewaele, 1998) and/or acquisition may be another factor affecting the performance of the L3 German learners. To them,

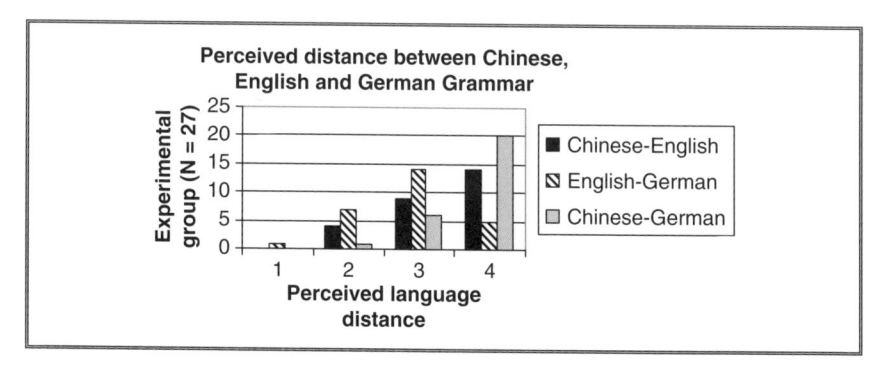

Figure 4.4 Perceived distance between Chinese, English and German grammar among the experimental participants (1 = Very close, 2 = Close, 3 = Different, 4 = Very different)

German is the most recently learned and used language, and this might affect their English.

According to one of the criteria in Andersen's (1983) 'Transfer to somewhere principle', transfer is likely to take place when a relevant structure is frequently found in the L1 and/or L2. Such a principle can also be extended to the L3. Since the German perfect is more frequently used in the spoken register than the preterite (Durrell, 2002: 295), some L3 German learners, possibly influenced by such frequent use in German and the overlap between German and English in indicating past time actions/events, would use the present perfect tense to indicate past situations in English.

The Role of L1 Chinese (Cantonese)

The nontarget use of the perfect is consistent with the influence from the L3 German tense/aspect system. In principle, such nontarget use could also result from L1 Chinese influence, such as interlingual identification with the Cantonese aspect marker *gwo3*.

Although *gwo3* seems to be a possible cause of L1 influence in the use of L2 English present perfect tense as discussed in the Section The Cantonese experiential aspect marker *gwo3*, none of the control group participants showed such influence in their narratives. On this basis, the 16 cases of nontarget use of the English present perfect tense in past situations among the experimental group are more likely to be the result of L3 German influence. The recency of use and/or acquisition and frequent use of German can, therefore, be viewed as underlying factors in influencing L2 English.

Conclusion

The results of the present study suggest that backward transfer may occur from L3 to L2 in certain areas of grammar. In other words, a later learned L3 can affect an earlier acquired L2. Some L3 German students were affected by the equivalence between the German preterite and perfect tenses and applied them in their L2 English writing. The higher mean ratings of the judgment task also show that the L3 German learners tended to accept nontarget English present perfect sentences more than the control group. The higher percentage of total acceptance (with a rating of '4') and the lower percentage of total rejection (with a rating of '1') of such ungrammatical sentences of the L3 German learners prove that their perception of the English present perfect tense was somewhat different from that of the controls. All these findings reveal that, in terms of the English tense usage, at least some L3 German learners were influenced by the formal and semantic overlap with the English present perfect. They extended the use of the English present perfect tense to include past situations without current relevance, just like the German perfect.

This demonstration of influence from L3 to L2 may have theoretical and applied implications. The backward transfer discussed in this study suggests a possible vulnerable domain (see Müller, 2003) in the learners' grammar. Further investigations are needed in order to have a clearer picture of the interlanguage involving an L3. In the meantime, English teachers can take note of such possible influence from another language, like German, and raise the awareness of their students about the overlapping between these two languages.

Notes

1. The possibility of transfer from L1 Chinese (Cantonese) to L2 English is addressed in the Section The Role of L1 Chinese (Cantonese).
2. One of the control participants, who participated in both tasks, had taken part in an exchange program to France for only three months and claimed that very little French was learned. As a result, this participant was included in the control group.
3. Two participants (one from each group) did not participate in the judgment task.
4. One control participant was excluded from the analysis because of an unanswered item.
5. Given the ambiguity, such cases are counted once only as examples of the nontarget use of the English present perfect tense.
6. The number in brackets is the number of L3 German learners choosing that option: 'always' (2), 'usually' (2), 'often' (6), 'sometimes' (10), 'seldom' (6) and 'never' (1).

References

Ahukanna, J.G.W., Lund, N.J. and Gentile, J.R. (1981) Inter- and intra-lingual interference effects in learning a third language. *The Modern Language Journal* 65 (3), 281–287.

Andersen, R.W. (1983) Transfer to somewhere. In S.M. Gass and L. Selinker (eds) *Language Transfer in Language Learning* (pp. 177–201). Rowley, MA: Newbury House.

Birdsong, D. (1989) *Metalinguistic Performance and Interlinguistic Competence*. Berlin: Springer-Verlag.

Bouvy, C. (2000) Towards the construction of a theory of cross-linguistic transfer. In J. Cenoz and U. Jessner (eds) *English in Europe: The Acquisition of a Third Language* (pp. 143–156). Clevedon: Multilingual Matters.

Cenoz, J., Hufeisen, B. and Jessner, U. (eds) (2001) *Cross-linguistic Influence in Third Language Acquisition: Psychological Perspectives*. Clevedon: Multilingual Matters.

Chuang, S-Y. (2002) *A Study of the Use of English Relative Clauses by Speakers of Chinese Learning German in Taiwan*. Unpublished MA thesis, University of Texas at Arlington, Arlington.

Comrie, B. (1985) *Tense*. Cambridge: Cambridge University Press.

De Angelis, G. (2007) *Third or Additional Language Acquisition*. Clevedon: Multilingual Matters.

De Angelis, G. and Selinker, L. (2001) Interlanguage transfer and competing linguistic systems in the multilingual mind. In J. Cenoz, B. Hufeisen and U. Jessner (eds) *Cross-linguistic Influence in Third Language Acquisition: Psychological Perspectives* (pp. 42–58). Clevedon: Multilingual Matters.
Dewaele, J-M. (1998) Lexical inventions: French interlanguage as L2 versus L3. *Applied Linguistics* 19 (4), 471–490.
Durrell, M. (2002) *Hammer's German Grammar and Usage* (4th edn). Chicago/London: McGraw-Hill.
Ellis, R. (1994) *The Study of Second Language Acquisition*. Oxford: Oxford University Press.
Ellis, R. (2008) *The Study of Second Language Acquisition* (2nd edn). Oxford: Oxford University Press.
Griessler, M. (2001) The effects of third language learning on second language proficiency: An Austrian example. *International Journal of Bilingual Education and Bilingualism* 4 (1), 50–60.
Hammarberg, B. (2009) Introduction. In B. Hammarberg (ed.) *Processes in Third Language Acquisition* (pp. 1–27). Edinburgh: Edinburgh University Press.
Huddleston, R.D. and Pullum, G.K. (2002) *The Cambridge Grammar of the English Language*. Cambridge: Cambridge University Press.
Jarvis, S. and Pavlenko, A. (2008) *Crosslinguistic Influence in Language and Cognition*. New York: Routledge.
Kellerman, E. (1977) Towards a characterization of the strategy of transfer in second language learning. *Interlanguage Studies Bulletin*, 2 (1), 58–145.
Matthews, S. and Yip, V. (1994) *Cantonese: A Comprehensive Grammar*. London: Routledge.
Müller, N. (ed.) (2003) *(In)vulnerable Domains in Multilingualism*. Amsterdam: John Benjamins.
Odlin, T. (1989) *Language Transfer: Cross-linguistic Influence in Language Learning*. Cambridge: Cambridge University Press.
Pavlenko, A. and Jarvis, S. (2002) Bidirectional transfer. *Applied Linguistics* 23 (2), 190–214.
Seliger, H.W. and Vago, R.M. (eds) (1991) *First Language Attrition*. Cambridge: Cambridge University Press.
Selinker, L. (1969) Language transfer. *General Linguistics* 9, 67–92.
Selinker, L. (1983) Language transfer. In S.M. Gass and L. Selinker (eds) *Language Transfer in Language Learning* (pp. 33–53). Rowley, MA: Newbury House.

Appendix A (Full List of Acceptability Judgment Sentences)

Ungrammatical present perfect

John has traveled to a number of European countries during the summer of 2007.

Yesterday, I have celebrated my friend's birthday with his parents.

My brother has paid a 100-dollar fine for his overdue books last week.

Last Christmas, I have received a pair of boots as a Christmas present.

While they were walking their dog this morning, they have witnessed a car accident.

Grammatical past

Did he work as a volunteer in the 2008 Beijing Olympic Games?
Jane's father taught her how to swim when she was ten years old.
Peter went to the cinema to watch the latest movie with his girlfriend last Sunday.
Last month I wrote a letter to my old classmate working in San Francisco.
During my visit to a dog center, I saw how puppies were trained to guide the blind.

Ungrammatical agreement

The girl who is holding a bouquet of flowers are one of my best friends.
Those comic books on the table was bought by my brother.
The workers' complaint about their salary are ignored by their employer.
He walk to school every day so that he can take more exercise.
Mary is a selfish child since she never share her toys with her little brother.

Grammatical agreement

My friends suggest that we should spend our holiday in a Southeast Asian country.
The children have already done all the housework for their sick mother.
The boy always shows off his large collection of model cars and trains to his friends.
I have changed the cage for my birds because the old one was too small.
The poor old man ran after the 50-cent coin that he had dropped from his purse.

Ungrammatical distractors

There are three ladies were wearing the same dress in tonight's party.
I'm sorry that I could not came to the meeting on Tuesday because I had a headache.
Tony is learning English, the world's lingua franca, since he was in the kindergarten.

Grammatical distractors

A stray cat is looking for food in the rubbish bin because it is hungry.
It is difficult to write different words with both hands at the same time.
Well-behaved students should pay attention to what the teacher says in class.

Chapter 5
Perception of Preposition Errors in Semantically Correct versus Erroneous Contexts by Multilingual Advanced English as a Foreign Language Learners: Measuring Metalinguistic Awareness

MARTHA GIBSON and BRITTA HUFEISEN

The present investigation had two aims. The first goal was to test findings and assumptions previously made about bilingual learners' superior metalinguistic abilities (see Bialystok, 1993, 2001, 2002). Bialystok's work with bilingual children has illustrated significant differences in two types of increased metalinguistic awareness (MLA). She divided these metalinguistic abilities into two kinds: *control of attention* and *analysis of structure*. Control of attention involves the capacity to detect and correct grammatical and semantic violations in the input. It includes the ability to focus attention on one feature of language, such as grammatical information, while at the same time ignoring a competing feature, such as the accompanying semantic information or meaning. This is demonstrated, for example, when native speakers of a language listen to a non-native speaker by ignoring or not consciously paying attention to any grammatical errors that the non-native speaker is making in order to concentrate on the content or intent of the message being communicated.

Bialystok's metalinguistically aware bilingual children respondents are able to do the opposite, that is, to ignore the semantic anomalies or nonsense in a target sentence and to accurately indicate whether the sentence is grammatically correct or incorrect. In her many investigations (Bialystok, 1988, 2001, *inter alia*), bilingual children show advantages over monolingual children in tasks that require high degrees of attention control, whereas on tasks that have high requirements for analysis of morpho-syntactic structure, this advantage over monolinguals is not apparent. She says that

[...] the effect of bilingualism on children's development is that it enhances their ability to attend to relevant information in the presence of misleading distractions. [...] It is only at the level of underlying processing that the pattern becomes clear. (Bialystok, 2001: 179)

Adult learners of a new language who already have experience in learning foreign languages (FLs) are just as aware that languages have, as termed by Eviatar and Ibrahim (2000: 454), an 'arbitrary nature', and thus that structures can be broken down and reorganized into other patterns. Thus, one would expect a positive relationship between a higher capacity of MLA and the ability to judge semantically anomalous sentences as grammatically correct or incorrect.

The second overall aim of this research was to test and verify claims made by researchers (Hufeisen, 2000a, 2000b, 2001; Hufeisen & Lindemann, 1998; Jessner, 1999, 2006; Kemp, 2007) that one of the salient qualitative differences between learners of a first FL and experienced learners of FLs consists of a greater depth and breadth in their metalinguistic abilities. Hufeisen's factor model in Figure 5.1 illustrates the basis for the cumulatively positive effect that multilingual learners will experience according to their level of MLA. Within the context of German (and German bilingual) university students learning English as a foreign language (EFL) in Germany, multilinguals with varying multilingual backgrounds have shown that having a higher number of FLs correlates positively with accuracy on a linguistic task with a high cognitive demand placed on explicit metalinguistic knowledge, that is, tasks requiring a high degree of structural analysis.

Neurophysiological Factors: General language acquisition capability, age, ...

Learner External Factors: Learning environment(s), type and amount of input...

Affective Factors: Motivation, (learning)anxiety, assessment of own language proficiency, perceived closeness/distance between the languages, attitude(s) towards languages, towards target cultures, towards languages learning, individual life experiences, ...

Cognitive Factors: Languages awareness, metalinguistic awareness, learning awareness, learner type awareness, learning strategies, individual learning experiences, ...

Foreign Language Specific Factors: Individual foreign language learning experiences and strategies, previous language interlanguages, interlanguage of target language(s), ...

Linguistic Factors: L1, L2, Lx, ...

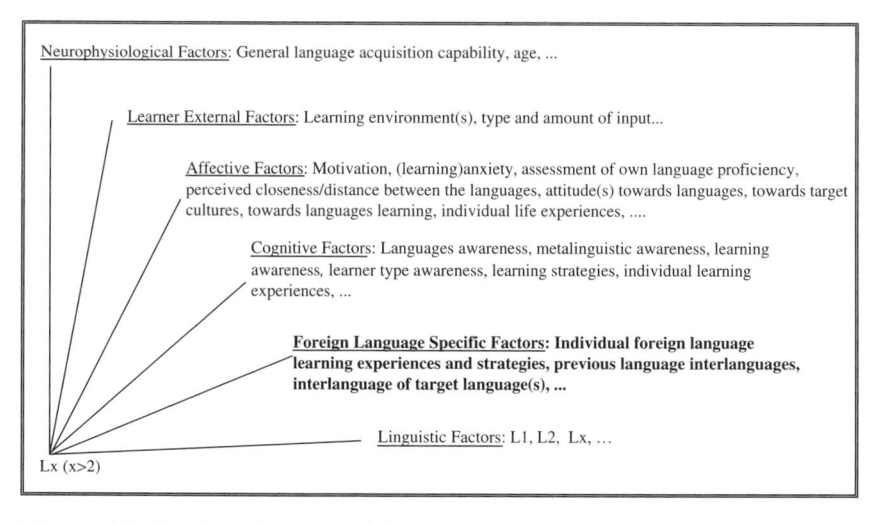

Lx (x>2)

Figure 5.1 Hufeisen factor model

The Study

The goal of the present study is to tap into and measure the greater amount of MLA that multilingual learners possess in a task that demands a high degree of attention to be paid to both grammatical and semantic correctness. In our overall conceptual question we ask: Will more experienced multilingual learners of English be better able to ignore distracting erroneous semantic information and correctly identify grammatically incorrect sentences than less experienced multilingual language learners?

Method

Participants

Our participants were all students at the *Technische Universität Darmstadt*, doing a joint Bachelor's degree in *Anglistik* (English Studies) and another field of study such as sociology, history or economics. All 47 participants were advanced-level EFL learners (high B2/low C1) taking part in a required English language course. These students all have German as their L1 or have been bilingual in German since babyhood. They ranged in multilingual background from having at least two previous FLs up to five previous FLs.

Stimuli

Participants were randomly assigned either task one or task two as a paper/pencil task to complete without an arbitrary time limit. The two tasks contained a made-up mini-mystery story containing eleven identical preposition errors. The preposition errors were chosen to present potential difficulties for these upper-intermediate to advanced EFL learners, particularly those with German as their L1. The prepositions *at* and *of* were taken as particular representatives of such problematic prepositions for even this group of advanced English learners. Task one was the *preposition error only* condition. Task one instructions, the story and the underlined target errors can be seen below. Prepositions that are not underlined served as distractor items in the task and were not included in the analysis.

Task one:

> The editors of the story below were having a very bad day and have left in many preposition errors. Please find as many errors as you can, underline/circle them and correct them. Then decide how seriously you think each grammatical error affects your understanding of the story on a scale of one to three, one = not at all seriously, two = somewhat seriously, three = very seriously.

A Murder Mystery

The dog was sitting near the lifeless body <u>from his master</u>, whose head lay <u>at a pool</u> of blood, with a handgun <u>at his lifeless hand</u>. Every time the detectives tried to get near the body, the dog would begin to growl and foam <u>on the mouth</u>. They finally had to call animal services to take the dog away. The victim had obviously been sitting <u>on his computer</u> when he died. Strangely enough, there was <u>no sign from</u> any bullet wounds on the victim. So how had he died? Where did the blood come from? He had obviously <u>died by something</u>, so the detectives carefully started to collect evidence <u>on the crime scene</u>. The revolver was tested for fingerprints and then put in a plastic bag. The blood <u>at the floor</u> was collected using a sponge. The half-eaten sandwich would be tested at the lab to see if the victim had possibly been poisoned in some way. Next they checked the story he had been <u>writing in his computer</u>. Could it have <u>a clue of the murderer</u> in it?

Error	*Your correction*	*Seriousness of Error*		
		Less <――― > More		
1. _____	_____	1	2	3
2. _____	_____	1	2	3
Etc.				

Task version two, the *preposition + semantic error* condition, contained the identical 11 target preposition errors, this time embedded in and surrounded by semantically nonsensical noun and verb phrases. Participants were explicitly directed to pay attention to the grammatical errors in this condition.

Task two:

> The writers of the story below were having a very bad day and not only wrote a silly story but left in many preposition errors. Please find as many preposition errors as you can, underline/circle them and correct them. Then decide how seriously you think each grammatical error affects your understanding of the story on a scale of one to three, one = not at all seriously, two = somewhat seriously, three = very seriously.

A Murder Mystery

The dog was reading near the lifeless body <u>from his master</u>, whose head lay <u>at a pool</u> of tennis balls, with a handgun <u>at his lifeless hand</u>. Every time the detectives tried to get near the body, the geranium would begin to growl and foam <u>on the mouth</u>. They finally had to call animal services to take the flower away. The victim had obviously been sitting <u>on his computer</u> when he died. Strangely enough, there was <u>no sign from</u> any bullet wounds on the victim. So how had he died? Where did the sunshine come from? He had obviously <u>died by something</u>, so the detectives carefully started to collect ice cream <u>on the crime scene</u>. The tiger was tested for fingerprints and then put in a plastic toy truck. The blood <u>at the floor</u> was collected using a pizza cutter. The half-eaten sandwich would be tested at the lab to see if the victim had possibly been hanged in some way. Next they checked the story he had been <u>writing in his computer</u>. Could it have <u>a clue of the murderer</u> in it?

Error	*Your correction*	*Seriousness of Error*		
		Less <		> More
1. _____	_____	1	2	3
2. _____	_____	1	2	3
Etc.				

Design

Our empirical framework combined a psycholinguistic-oriented methodology (i.e. paper/pencil questionnaire) with the applied goal of adding to the body of knowledge about the learning/processing of preposition systems by EFL learners. Our specific empirical questions and expectations broke down as follows:

(1) Will participants with a greater number of previous FLs be able to identify errors more accurately in the *semantic + preposition errors task* than participants with fewer FLs?

This first question focuses on assessing the overall assumption that experienced FL learners possess a higher degree of MLA than inexperienced FL learners (Hufeisen, 1998, 2001; Jessner, 2003, 2006, *inter alia*). The second assumption is that having a greater degree of MLA will translate into a higher grammatical accuracy score on the error task.

Our first expectation was that all participants would perform more accurately overall on the task containing *preposition errors only* than on the task with both *semantic + preposition errors*. In line with previous research findings, as discussed in the introduction, there should be a greater cognitive burden placed on a participant's attention, focusing resources when semantic misinformation is present, thereby lowering accuracy scores.

Our second expectation was that the more FLs the participants had at their disposal, the more success they would have in the task that included both semantic and preposition errors compared with participants with fewer previous FLs. Experienced language learners are expected to be better able to ignore the distracting erroneous semantic content in the task, given their broader experience with extracting meaning from various forms and systems of language input. Another advantage that the more experienced FL learners should show in the task also pertains to their ability to discern and deal with erroneous semantic information in the message, provided by a more developed degree of MLA. An enhanced 'ability to attend to relevant information in the presence of misleading distractions' (Bialystok, 2001: 179) is essentially being tested with regard to multilinguals. One possible result in the present investigation is that possessing a greater degree of MLA will allow these participants to pay more and more discrete attention to the more salient (i.e. semantically erroneous) output. Thus, more experienced FL learners should show themselves by judging errors as less serious in the *semantic + preposition errors* task when compared with learners with fewer FLs and therefore lower MLA.

(2) Will participants who know a greater number of previous FLs judge preposition errors in the *preposition errors only task* as more 'serious' than participants with fewer FLs?

This second question is intended to determine whether participants with a differing numbers of FLs will behave differently in their error severity judgements when only a grammatical error is involved. In a previous investigation (Gibson & Hufeisen, 2007), more experienced multilingual participants (i.e. who knew more FLs) tended to judge errors involving the English preposition *of* more harshly or seriously than did those participants with fewer FLs. It is, therefore, possible that this result will be replicated when the linguistic input contains an even wider range of spatial preposition errors, including *at, on, in* and *of*.

Results

The 11 target preposition errors were correctly identified with means of 70% and 64% in the *preposition errors only* task and the *preposition + semantic errors* task, respectively. Scores for each target error are specified in Table 5.1 and range from 8% to 92% over both tasks. In the case of the lowest accuracy score of 8% and 22%, it appears likely that the lower lexical frequency of the accompanying noun phrase *clue to* affected the accuracy score for this preposition error in both tasks. In addition, the preposition *of* itself could also have negatively contributed to accuracy levels. *Of* tends to be a tricky English preposition for German speakers to master, partly because in German *von* (*from*) subsumes the possessive/linking meaning expressed in English by *of*. This preposition was therefore eliminated from the final data analysis, leaving a total of

Table 5.1 Target preposition accuracy scores (%)

	Preposition error	*Correct preposition*	*Percentage prep errors only task*	*Correct semantic + prep errors task*
1	*at* a pool of blood	in/by	92	70
2	*from* his master	of	88	70
3	*in* his computer	on/at	79	83
4	*at* the floor	on	83	74
5	*on* his computer	at	79	74
6	*at* his hand	in	79	70
7	*from* any wound	of	71	57
8	foaming *on* the mouth	at/from	63	61
9	died *by* something	of/from	67	48
10	*on* the crime scene	at	58	78
			Mean = 76%	**Mean = 69%**
*11	clue *of* the murderer	to	8	22

10 target preposition errors, resulting in correct mean scores of 76% (SD = 10.9) on the *preposition errors only* task and 69% (SD = 10.4) on the *preposition + semantic errors* task.

Effects of task

Data from two participants were eliminated from the final analysis since they clearly did not complete the task properly, leaving a total of 24 participants in the *preposition errors only* task and 23 in the *semantic + preposition errors* task.

A two-tailed independent samples *t*-test conducted on how well the remaining 45 participants scored showed that there was no significant difference in the mean accuracy scores on the 10 prepositions over the two tasks, $t(18) = 0.039$, $p < 0.14$, SD = 2.7, SE = 4.77. In other words, accurately identifying the errors in the *preposition errors only* task was not significantly easier or harder for participants than in the *semantic + preposition errors* task, with mean scores of 7.6 out of 10 and 7.2 out of 10, respectively. In other words, the semantically anomalous information did not overly negatively influence the ability of participants to pay attention to the grammatically incorrect information.

Effect of foreign languages

Task accuracy

In terms of accuracy scores, two independent samples *t*-tests found no significant difference between the two tasks (*preposition errors only*, $N = 24$, $M = 7.66$, SD = 1.85, versus *semantic + preposition errors*, $N = 21$, $M = 7.42$, SD = 2.16); $t(43) = 0.398$, $p = 0.69$).

Given the very small Ns for participants in each of the four levels of FLs, ranging from five participants with five or more FLs to a high of 18 participants with three FLs, we decided to collapse this variable into two levels, dividing participants into two groups, with 'more' ($n = 32$) versus 'less' ($n = 13$) FL experience. We were interested in whether this more basic distinction would reveal any insight into the abilities of the very experienced multilingual participants compared with less-experienced multilinguals. We assumed once again that the ability of participants to accurately find and correct preposition errors overall should be positively related to how much experience they have had in learning FLs.

In a two-way independent samples *t*-test, the amount of FL experience turned out to be significant. Having more than two FLs resulted in a mean accuracy score of 7.97 (SD = 1.95, SE = 0.346) and having two FLs 'only' resulted in a mean accuracy score of 6.54 (SD = 1.71, SE = 0.475). The *t*-score was $t(43) = -1.43$, $p < 0.027$. That is, the 'less' experienced FL learners (2 FLs) did significantly less well in finding and correcting the preposition errors over both tasks compared to the 'super' experienced FL learners. This result is illustrated in Figure 5.2.

Error severity judgements

In terms of error severity judgments, it turned out that 'less' experienced multilingual participants rated the preposition errors over both tasks as slightly more serious overall than did the 'more' experienced participants, with means of 2.08 out of 3 versus 1.83 out of 3 (see

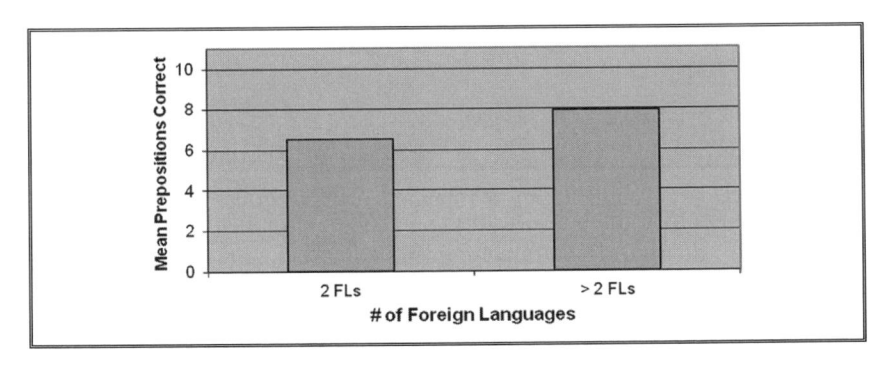

Figure 5.2 Number of foreign languages and overall task accuracy

Figure 5.3). A one-sample Kolmogorov-Smirnov test indicated that the distribution of error severity scores was normal with a mean of 1.907 and a standard deviation of 0.46, $p = 0.725$. This difference is non-significant at the 0.05 level.

An interesting significant relationship was found between participants having two, three, four or five previous FLs and how often they rated the preposition errors as *least serious, serious* and *most serious*. It turned out that the more language knowledge a participant had, the less severely s/he tended to judge the preposition errors over both tasks (df = 6, $N = 45$, $\chi^2 = 20.25$, $p < 0.003$). The observed frequencies for the error severity judgements within the four levels of FL knowledge are illustrated in Figure 5.4.

It is readily apparent that the middle of the scale, 2 (*serious*), was by far the most common judgement, even though participants were reminded

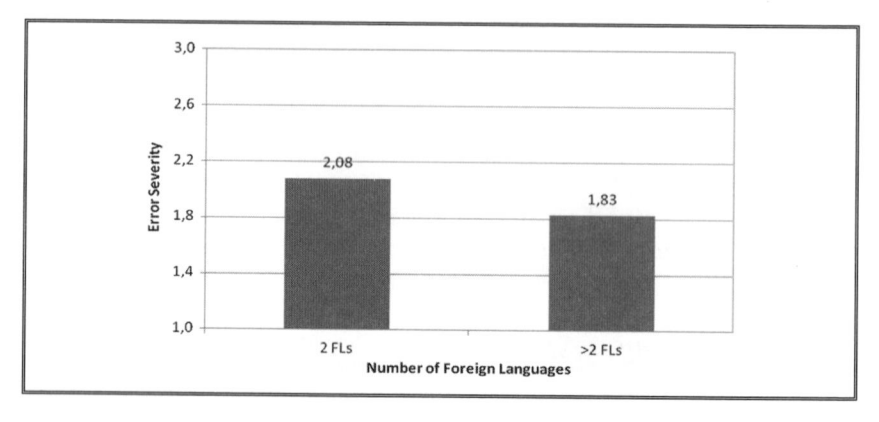

Figure 5.3 Error severity judgement means by number of foreign languages (2 levels) over both tasks ($N = 45$)

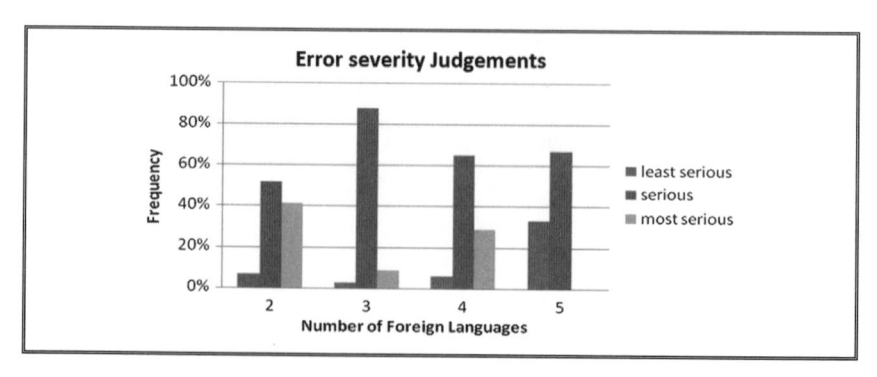

Figure 5.4 Error severity judgements by number of foreign languages ($N = 45$)

verbally to use the whole scale in their assessments. Notwithstanding, an interesting behaviour pattern that emerged here is that the most experienced multilinguals, those with five previous FLs, judged none (0%) of the preposition errors as *most serious*, whereas the least experienced multilinguals, those with two FLs, considered 41% of the errors to fall into the *most serious* category. The opposite pattern held for *least serious* errors, such that the least experienced multilinguals considered very few errors (7%) to be *least serious*, whereas the most experienced multilinguals classified 33% of the target errors as *least serious*.

A χ^2 was also used to check whether the proportions of participants judging errors from least to most serious was significantly related to the task type, *preposition errors only* versus *semantic + preposition errors*. No statistical significance was found for this comparison (2, $N = 45$, $\chi^2 = 1.48$, $p = 0.48$). This result confirmed that the amount of nonsensical linguistic input in the task was not making a significant impact on the way participants were processing the preposition errors in the task.

Discussion

Our investigation was designed to assess how a multilingual's increased experience with FLs would affect two tasks: first, error identification and correction, and second, the perceived effect of such errors on the comprehensibility of a text. The first task was a typical linguistic task, and our results reinforced our assumption from previous research (see discussion in introduction) that more FL experience translates into more efficient linguistic abilities at the grammatical level, particularly when considering the super-experienced multilinguals in our study, compared to the less-experienced multilinguals. It must also be kept in mind when considering the results of our study that our multilingual experimental group included a number of super-experienced FL learners or multilinguals in an academic setting and that this population might not be representative of a 'typical' adult FL learner group.

The second task of judging the seriousness/severity of a grammatical error was meant to investigate the assumption in numerous multilingual research studies that experienced multilinguals also have a concomitant advantage in their MLA abilities compared with less-experienced multilinguals. Our results partially confirmed this expectation in that the very experienced multilinguals seemed to be processing the severity of preposition errors in an FL differently from less-experienced multilinguals. The trend was for less experienced multilinguals to judge more errors as *most serious*, a category that the most-experienced multilinguals made no use of, and instead, considered many more errors to be in the *least serious* category. This latter category was, in turn, not favoured by the least experienced multilinguals in their judgements. These contrastive perceptual behaviours could be interpreted variously. The difference could be evidence that the super multilinguals in the study have a less harsh or more tolerant view of grammatical errors when occurring in one of their many FLs. Or they might simply be focusing on the message more than on the errors overall. However, since there was no significant difference between the two task types in our study, only a trend for lower accuracy and higher severity judgments in the *semantic + preposition errors* task, this notion needs more systematic study.

Nevertheless, what is clear from this study is that very experienced multilinguals are able to detect and correct preposition errors more accurately than less experienced learners when the English proficiency levels of the participants is kept constant. There is also a trend for very experienced multilinguals to be less harsh in their condemnation of the preposition errors in both meaningful and nonsensical contexts than are the less-experienced FL learners. Multilinguals at the two ends of the scale in the study, two versus five FLs, are possibly employing more or different metalinguistic strategies than their less-experienced counterparts. The perceptual behaviour of these two extreme groups, as well as a closer investigation of the two middle groups, those with three and four FLs, requires further study, perhaps one that targets metalinguistic abilities by more sharply differentiating between sensical and nonsensical linguistic input.

References

Bialystok, E. (1988) Aspects of linguistic awareness in reading comprehension. *Applied Psycholinguistics* 9, 123–139.
Bialystok, E. (1993) Symbolic representation and attentional control in pragmatic competence. In G. Kaspar and S. Blum-Kulka (eds) *Interlanguage Pragmatics* (pp. 43–63). Oxford: Oxford University Press.
Bialystok, E. (2001) Metalinguistic aspects of bilingual processing. *Annual Review of Applied Linguistics* 21, 169–181.
Bialystok, E. (2002) Cognitive processes of L2 users. In V. Cook (ed.) *Portraits of the L2 User* (pp. 145–166). Clevedon: Multilingual Matters.
Eviatar, Z. and Ibrahim, R. (2000) Bilingual is as bilingual does: Metalinguistic abilities of Arabic-speaking children. *Applied Psycholinguistics* 21, 451–471.
Gibson, M. and Hufeisen, B. (2007) Usage judgements of OF by multilingual learners of English. Paper presented at *Fifth International Conference on Third Language Acquisition and Multilingualism*, University of Stirling September 3–5, 2007.
Hufeisen, B. (1998) L3-Stand der Forschung – Was bleibt zu tun? In B. Hufeisen and B. Lindemann (eds) *Tertiärsprachen, Theorien, Modelle, Methoden* (pp. 169–183). Tübingen: Stauffenburg
Hufeisen, B. (2000a) A European perspective – Tertiary languages with a focus on German as L3. In J.W. Rosenthal (ed.) *Handbook of Undergraduate Second Language Education: English as a Second Language, Bilingual and Foreign language*

Instruction for a Multilingual World (pp. 209–229). Mahwah NJ: Lawrence Erlbaum.
Hufeisen, B. (2000b) How do foreign language learners evaluate various aspects of their multilingualism? In B. Hufeisen and B. Lindemann (eds) *Tertiär-und Drittsprachen* (pp. 23–40). Tübingen: Stauffenburg.
Hufeisen, B. (2001) Deutsch als Tertiä rsprache. In G. Helbig, L. Götze, G. Henrici and H.J. Krumm (eds) *Deutsch als Fremdsprache. Ein internationales Handbuch* (pp. 648–653). Berlin: Walter de Gruyter.
Hufeisen, B. and Lindemann, B. (1998) *Tertiärsprachen. Theorien, Modelle, Methoden.* Tübingen: Stauffenburg.
Jessner, U. (1999) Metalinguistic awareness in multilinguals: Cognitive aspects of third language learning. *Language Awareness* 8 (3 and 4), 201–209.
Jessner, U. (2003) On the nature of crosslinguistic interaction in multilinguals. In J. Cenoz, B. Hufeisen and U. Jessner (eds) *The Multilingual Lexicon* (pp. 45–55). Dordrecht: Kluwer.
Jessner, U. (2006) *Linguistic Awareness in Multilinguals. English as a Third Language.* Edinburgh: Edinburgh University Press.
Kemp, C. (2007) Strategic processing in grammar learning: Do multilinguals use more strategies? *International Journal of Multilingualism* 4 (4), 241–261.

Chapter 6
'Luisa and Pedrito's Dog will the Breakfast Eat': Interlanguage Transfer and the Role of the Second Language Factor

LAURA SANCHEZ

Introduction

Probably the most characteristic feature of *third or additional language acquisition* (TLA), understood here as the acquisition of 'all languages beyond the L2 without giving preference to any particular language' (De Angelis, 2007: 11), is the simultaneous operation of various factors at a single point in time (e.g. '(psycho)typology', 'L2 status', 'proficiency', 'recency' of acquisition, 'frequency of use' and 'chronological order' or sequence of acquisition of the different languages of a multilingual speaker). The relevance of the concurrent effects of these factors (Cenoz *et al.*, 2001a, 2001b, 2003) has become evident in a number of empirical studies with multilinguals, particularly those with an explicit focus on non-native language influence (e.g. Abunuwara, 1992; Afganova, 1997; Chandrasekhar, 1978; Christen & Näf, 2001; De Angelis, 2005; De Angelis & Selinker, 2001; Dentler, 2000; Dewaele, 1998; Hufeisen, 1991; Ilomaki, 2005; Lindemann, 2000; Michiels, 1999; Möhle, 1989; Müller-Lancé, 2003a, 2003b; Ringbom, 1982, 1987; Selinker & Baumgartner-Cohen, 1995; Singleton, 1987; Stedje, 1977; Vogel, 1992; Welge, 1987; Wode *et al.*, 1992). This is particularly the case for two factors that appear to be in constant rivalry, namely, (psycho)typology and L2 status. The rivalry between these has divided the research community into advocates of theoretical stances defending one factor or the other. A short time ago, Singleton and Ó'Laoire (2006) referred to these as the *psychotypological perspective* and the *L2 factor perspective*. The following paragraphs discuss the role of these factors on the basis of existing empirical evidence and speculate on the tentative conclusions reached in some studies.

Although a large body of literature has addressed typological issues for several decades, research on L2 status has a short history. Because of its very nature, this factor (which has also been referred to in the literature as 'the second language factor', 'the L2 factor' or the factor 'status of the interlanguage') is exclusive to TLA. Pioneer work by Hammarberg (2001), Williams and Hammarberg (1993, 1998) and other authors (e.g. Dewaele, 1998; Shanon, 1991) has called attention to the importance of its effects on TLA. Despite repeated mention of this factor, an operationalised definition has not been offered until recently. To my knowledge, the most recent operationalisation is that by Leung, who implies that

> The 'second language (L2) factor' in L3 acquisition refers to the general tendency to *transfer* (representations) from L2(s) rather than L1. In online processing/ performance terms, 'L2 status' is usually used to express the idea of general tendency to activate L2(s) rather than the L1. (Leung 2007: 102)

Crucially, this factor is important in itself and also as regards its complex relations with other factors. Bardel and Lindqvist (2007: 127), for example, put forward that 'in the choice between L1 and L2, L2 status *per se* seems to be an important factor'. Furthermore, it seems to have been effectively demonstrated that L2 status is decisive in determining the *degree* or *level* of activation of each of the languages in the linguistic repertoire of the learner and their influence on the acquisition of a subsequent non-native language (e.g. Bardel & Lindqvist, 2007; De Angelis, 2007; De Angelis & Selinker, 2001; de Bot, 2004; Dewaele, 1998; Hammarberg, 2001; Leung, 2007, 2008; Williams & Hammarberg, 1998). For this reason, in addition to the first definition of transfer in Odlin (1989), the core notion of transfer has been revisited and redefined in order to embrace the kind of language interaction typical of language acquisition in multilingual contexts. Some instances of this are Bouvy's (2000) and Cenoz's (2000) *crosslinguistic transfer*, described as 'largely an unconscious interaction phenomenon between evolving sets of imperfectly acquired structures' (Bouvy, 2000: 143). Herdina and Jessner (2002; see also Jessner, 2008) coined the term CLIN or *crosslinguistic interaction* to refer to the different kinds of influences that can occur in multilinguals. However, the most precise and exact term to refer, specifically, to the influence of a non-native language upon another non-native language is that of *interlanguage transfer*, coined by De Angelis (1999, 2005, 2007) and defined as 'the transfer from one interlanguage to another'[1] (De Angelis & Selinker, 2001: 43). De Angelis (2007) claims that *interlanguage transfer* is based on the so-called 'difference assumption', according to which there is a fundamental difference between the acquisition of a *first* non-native language and that of a *second* non-native language, that is, between an L2 and an L3. The critical difference then is between the acquisition of an L2 and an L3 but not between an L3 and an L4, an L5 and so on, as Hufeisen (2003) had already anticipated (see also Hammarberg, 2009a, 2009b, and Köberle, 1998).

In turn, the typology factor in TLA (e.g. Foote, 2009; Ringbom, 2001), or *psychotypology* factor (Kellerman, 1983), when it refers to learners' perception of the typological closeness or distance between languages, is worthy of note for many reasons including that it is believed to foster cross-language competition, at least at the level of lexis. After all, Odlin notes,

> In any learner's attempt to acquire a new language, language distance is ultimately in the eye of the beholder. Research indicates that when everything is equal, transfer will most likely result from a learner's judgement (made consciously or unconsciously) that particular structures in a previously learned language are quite like – if not the same as – structures in the target language. (Odlin, 1989: 142)

Because of the intricate ways in which all these factors interact, the central dimension in research on crosslinguistic influence in TLA is precisely between (psycho)typology and L2 status. When it comes to the above-mentioned rivalry, Singleton and Ó'Laoire claim that the debate is

> on the question of whether the critical factor in the resorting to language *y* when using language *z* is (a) that the language user perceives language *y* as typologically closer to language *z* than any other available language or (b) that language *y* is, in common with language *z*, a non-native language. (Singleton & Ó'Laoire, 2006: 192)

The complexity of the interplay of factors is remarkably manifest as far as typology is concerned. Research in TLA provides strong evidence against the investigation of the typology factor in isolation (which may present only a partial or incomplete view of the picture). A great case in point is the interrelationship between typology and proficiency in all the languages of the multilingual (Hammarberg, 2001, 2009a; Jaensch, 2009; Tremblay, 2006; Williams & Hammarberg, 1993, 1998). In their investigation of a Swedish adult learner of Italian with prior knowledge of English, French and Spanish, Bardel and Lindqvist (2007: 138) found that the effects of typology were overridden by those of proficiency, since they observed that 'the proficiency factor rules out the psychotypology factor in the choice between French and Spanish'. Besides, another drawback in the explanatory power of (psycho)typology in TLA is that it has often been investigated in situations where the L1 is typologically distant from both the L2 and the L3 (e.g. Ahukana *et al.*, 1981; Chumbow, 1981; Hufeisen, 1993; Sikogurika, 1993; Singh & Carroll, 1979). In such scenarios, it is difficult to ascertain whether L2 influence (or lack thereof) is due to the no operability of L2 status or because the L1 falls short of sufficient comparable linguistic material to draw from.

Consequently, claims on the effects of typological similarities and differences (particularly *positive*, but also negative) must be viewed with caution. As Cenoz (2003: 104, emphasis added) judiciously points out, *'languages are relatively distant or relatively close, not distant or close in absolute terms'*. She further argues that, for example, Spanish can be considered distant from English if compared with Dutch but closer to English if compared to Japanese. Thus, the consideration of actual distance in 'relative' terms has got important psycholinguistic implications. If the languages in a given combination are considered to be relatively distant, then important differences might be found at the lexeme and the lemma levels, which in turn, would lead to stronger effects for the typology factor than for L2 status. Likewise, Bardel and Lindqvist (2007: 139, emphasis added) hold that 'the typological relationship between Spanish and Italian plays a role, not only in a *general* sense as language systems, but above all at the phonological level'. Still, they suggest, 'the Romance languages resemble each other to a different extent at different linguistic levels' (Bardel & Lindqvist, 2007: 130). As a result, French and Spanish (closely related to each other from the point of view of lexis and grammar) could, in principle, be perceived as closer to Italian than to English or Swedish. Alternatively, though, it might also be possible that 'English could be regarded as closer to the Romance languages than Swedish, particularly as far as lexis is concerned' (Bardel & Lindqvist, 2007: 130).

Along similar lines, the need to deal with typological effects in relative terms is also underscored elsewhere. Tracy and Gawlitzek-Maiwald contend that 'in view of what Clyne (1987) referred to as "grey areas" between languages, separability and independence *may not be an all-or-nothing issue* but rather involve iterative problem solving' (Tracy & Gawlitzek-Maiwald 2005: 28, emphasis added). Moreover, the authors sustain that the ability to keep linguistic systems apart is very much dependent upon the similarities and differences between their subsystems. It is basically at this point that the role of psychotypology becomes more important. Ringbom (2007, 2009) argues that it may be because of psychotypology that learners happen to extend actual similarities in a given area or subsystem of language to other subsystems. To put it another way, psychotypology might eventually lead them to wrongly assume similarities (or differences) where they do not exist objectively (see also Jarvis & Pavlenko, 2008). In sum, the evidence discussed here points to inconclusive results (sometimes even contradictory). From this, it follows that further research is needed without delay, with the hope that it will be of assistance in clarifying the roles of the two factors under examination here.

The Study

The study[2] presented here is part of a larger investigation on the effects of age and input by the GRAL Research Group.[3] In particular, this part of the study relied on data from pre-pubertal learners and attempted to shed light on the yet unresolved issue of the roles of the *psychotypological perspective* and the *L2 factor perspective* in explaining interlanguage transfer in TLA. To do so, the focus of the study was the influence of an L3 German on *ab initio* L4 English primary school learners who were bilingual in Spanish and Catalan. The methodological research design of the empirical study reported here made it possible to look at the two factors separately. This is so because, although all the languages in the present study are reasonably equidistant, the L3 was *relatively distant* from the L1, L2 and L4 in the linguistic level selected for analysis (namely, syntax and verb placement), as we will see in the following section.

Rationale of the Study and Hypotheses

The research question of the study relates to the respective roles of the factors of typology and L2 status in the occurrence of *interlanguage transfer* in an L4 (English). In particular, in order to account for the explanatory power of each factor, it asked whether typological closeness between the L1 Spanish, L2 Catalan and L4 English might prevent the activation of L3 German syntax during L4 production. This question was put forward on the assumption that the effects of L2 status may eventually be stronger than those of typology or, at least, that the typological differences between L3 German and L4 English at the level of syntax may not be sufficient to prevent activation of L3 German during production in L4 English. This is so, despite the objective similarities between the L1, the L2 and the L4 in the linguistic level examined. In other words, the contention here is that beyond these similarities, the effect of the L2 status factor will promote activation of a prior non-native language and interlanguage transfer.

Participants

To answer this question, data were collected from 154 simultaneous bilinguals (Spanish and Catalan) from birth. They were learning German as L3 in a context of partial immersion that combined formal instruction with (occasionally) naturalistic exposure. They were also learning English as L4 only through formal instruction at school, that is, they were receiving no extracurricular exposure to this language outside the school context.

Table 6.1 Participating groups

Group	N	Mean age	L3 intensity of exposure	L3 Instructional time
EG3	17	8–9	1 h/w	33 h
EG4	62	9–10	1 h/w	33 h
EG5(A)	34	10–11	1 h/w	66 h
EG5(B)	41	10–11	2 h/w	99 h

The sample included data from learners aged 8.9–10.9 years. In particular, they were third graders (EG3), fourth graders (EG4) and fifth graders (EG5A, EG5B). Third and fourth graders were receiving 1 hour of instruction a week in the L4 at the time of data collection, and their instructional time had accumulated 33 hours of instruction. Fifth graders were further subdivided into two groups (EG5A, EG5B) that differed in intensity of instruction (one vs. two weekly hours of instruction) and also in average instructional time in the L3 English (i.e. 66 and 99 hours). Thus, all participants were tested before the sensitive period for the acquisition of morphosyntax (namely, around the mid-teens, according to Birdsong, 1992; DeKeyser, 2000; DeKeyser & Larson-Hall, 2005; Larson-Hall, 2008; Patkowski, 1980; White & Genesee, 1996) and had received less than 100 hours of instruction in this language. The information of the experimental groups participating in the study is summarized in Table 6.1.

Elicitation Procedure

The instrument used in the data collection was a story telling task called 'The Dog Story' (see Appendix) in its written modality, which was adapted from a narrative picture story in Heaton (1966). It is part of the battery of tests in use in the GRAL Research Group, and it has been extensively employed in the Barcelona Age and Input Factors Project, in particular. Indeed, narratives elicited using this story form an important part of the Barcelona English Language Corpus (BELC).[4] In relation to the visual stimuli, the picture series comprised six panels, and the plot of the story was described by Muñoz in the following way: 'There are two main protagonists, a boy and a girl, who are getting ready for a picnic; a secondary character, their mother; and a character that disappears and later reappears, a dog that gets into the food basket and eats the children's sandwiches' (Muñoz, 2006: 21). The decision to use this task was motivated by its suitability for the investigation of transfer (Sanchez & Jarvis, 2008) and because it involves a language-specific processing mode. As such (in contrast to other elicitation techniques), this task was supposed to minimize non-target language activation because, since it is language-specific, it should require the activation of *only* the intended language.

The task was time-controlled (15 minutes). It was not familiar to the learners, and it was administered in class to all intact groups. They were given a sheet with the six pictures of the story and a separate white sheet on which to write the story. The participants were not allowed to ask questions related to the vocabulary of the story or to use a dictionary, grammar book, or similar reference tools. They were instructed to not describe the pictures but, rather, to try and explain the story as a whole. They were explicitly informed that the test would not count as a class score. The activity was carried out under the supervision of their teacher and the researcher (in this case, the author of this study). Learners had no time preparation, but they had the series of pictures in front of them while doing the task.

Data Analysis

The two non-native languages in the present study were both Germanic languages (L3 German and L4 English). Notwithstanding, they show essential typological differences as regards Verb-Object (VO) and Object-Verb (OV) orders in some constructions. These differences are critical here because L3 German presents a structural contrast in this particular domain with respect to the L1s and the L4 in that Spanish, Catalan and English are VO languages. The most representative linguistic properties of German verb placement are presented in Table 6.2. For the present purposes, the linguistic analysis will concentrate solely on the *Rule of Discontinuous Verb Placement* in main clauses and *Verb Final* in subordinate clauses with simple verb phrases.

The whole pool of data was checked in order to identify *empirically relevant contexts*, that is, those that allowed an examination of the investigation of interlanguage transfer. These were main clauses with complex verb phrases and subordinate clauses with simple verb phrases. After that, the occurrence of transferred orders (i.e. OV orders in empirically relevant contexts) was quantified and submitted to statistical treatment.

Results

Qualitative results

After this, the *qualitative* analysis of the data showed that L3 German was highly activated during L4 English production. In light of the complement–verb orders observed in the L4 English interlanguage of the learners, activation of the L3 was seen in the interlanguage transfer of OV orders in main clauses supplied in the L4 that resulted from the application of the L3 'rule of discontinuous verb placement'. For the

'Luisa and Pedrito's Dog will the Breakfast Eat'

Table 6.2 Linguistic properties of verb placement in L3 German

Linguistic property	Clause category	Description
(a) Inversion rule (INV)	Main	Subject–Verb Inversion When the subject does not occupy the first position in the clause
(b) Rule of discontinuous verb placement (SEP)	Main	The finite verb occupies the second position in the clause (V2) and the non-finite verb occupies the last position in the clause
(c) Verb particle[5] constructions (VPCs)	Main/Sub.	In main clauses, the verb occupies the second position in the clause (V2) and the particle occupies the last position. In subordinate clauses, the finite verb appears at the end, preceded by the particle.
(d) Verb final (VFINAL)	Sub.	The verb always appears at the end of the clause. In complex verb constructions, the non-finite form precedes the finite form
(e) Adverb placement (ADV)	Main/Sub.	Scrambling (S-V-O-A and S-V-A-O)

sake of clarity, the examples below are classified into two data sets. The first set takes account of interlanguage transfer of this rule in constructions where tense auxiliaries were used. To be more precise, (1) to (4) display the use of OV orders in secondary tenses (that is, those tenses that do not show inflectional distinctions and mark tense by means of an auxiliary). The orderings in L4 English interlanguage affected by influence of L3 German appear in italics:

(1) The dog *have* the picnic *ating*
(2) He *has* a picknick *eating*
(3) The dog *have* the breakfast *eat*
(4) Peter and Laura *have* not the breakfast *eats*

Other constructions involving the use of tense auxiliaries that suggest evidence of interlanguage transfer in the area examined are the following:

(5) The dog *is* the brekfast *eat*
(6) They *is* the food *eating*
(7) The dog *are* the sandwiches *eating*
(8) And her dog *is* the food ~~ge~~ ~~eat~~ *eating*

The second set took in data that called for the use of modality-bearing modal auxiliaries and future-referring auxiliaries. Mood here is understood as a grammatical form that expresses the semantic category of 'modality' in lexical means (that is, by using modal auxiliaries) and as a grammatical form that expresses futurity. The semantic distinction between 'modality' and 'futurity' is based on Huddleston and Pullum (2006: 56) who, in spite of this distinction (the auxiliary 'will' is regarded both grammatically and semantically as a *mood marker* rather than a *tense marker*), see an 'intrinsic connection between future time and modality'. The use of L2-induced OV orders with these kinds of auxiliaries is illustrated in (9)–(12). Following Gawlitzek-Maiwald (2000: 129), 'want' was treated as a modal verb for the purpose of classification (as for example in 9 below). According to her, in cases such as *now I want a chimney builden* (produced by a German–English bilingual child), the 'verb *want* receives the subcategorisation frame of the German modal verb *wollen*; thus, it combines with a VP and with a finite subordinate clause or an IC as required by want'. This argument is further supported by the fact that 'the structure of the VP is German although the lexical items are English'.

(9) They *want* a picknik *meik*
(10) Janet and Pedro *must* the breakfast *doing*
(11) Luisa and Pedrito's dog *will* the breakfast *eat*
(12) but the dog Rex *will* with Joe and Anna *going*

The same kind of interlanguage transfer was observed as well in subordinate clauses. The activation of L3 German resulted in the transfer of the 'verb final' rule in this clause type, as can be inferred from the instances in 13 to 16 here:

(13) because the dog the sandwitch *eating*
(14) when the dog the sandwiches *eat*
(15) when Susi a man *write*
(16) When they with the mum *talk*

Although these (13–16) illustrate OV orders with lexical verbs, examples (17) to (20) do so for subordinate clauses with a copula:

(17) When the two brothers in the piknik *are*
(18) When their in the Camp *are*
(19) When they in the mountains *were*
(20) that Bello with them *are*

Quantitative results

The kind of interlanguage transfer explained in the preceding section was quantified and introduced in the SPSS software (Statistical Package for the social sciences, Version 16) for its statistical treatment. In order to have as clear a picture as possible, the first step prior to this was to differentiate from the total number of participants those who created empirically relevant contexts and those who did not. The results indicated that 86 out of the 154 learners participating in the study (that is, nearly 56% of them against 68 learners or 44%) *did* create empirically relevant contexts in the means and ways described in Qualitative results. The next step was to estimate the occurrence of interlanguage transfer in learners who created empirically relevant contexts. Subsequent analyses were performed only on data from these 86 learners, which constituted the working sample for the rest of the analyses. This sample was then checked again with the aim of inquiring into the representativity of interlanguage transfer from L3 German in L4 English interlanguage.

It was found that, in broad terms, 89.5% of the working sample transferred and only 10.5% did not. A closer look at the distribution of interlanguage transfer in the linguistic properties examined here revealed that learners transferred the L3 German rule of discontinuous verb placement in main clauses on 95% of the occasions.[6] The overall representativity of interlanguage transfer in main clauses with discontinuous verb placement was extremely high, namely, 95% of occurrences. More precisely, the distribution of transferred OV orders in clauses with *tense* and *modal* auxiliaries was 94.9% and 95.5%, respectively. In subordinate clauses, the percentage of transfer of the L3 verb final rule was 85.4%. When all the contexts in the main and subordinate clauses were considered together, interlanguage transfer represented 92.6% of the total number of empirically relevant contexts (i.e. 149 over 161). The rate of occurrence shown by these figures is presented in Table 6.3, where these are set out in full in raw numbers and percentages.

In order to inquire into the systematicity of transferred orders within each participant, the internal consistency of interlanguage transfer was investigated in the different linguistic properties that constitute the focus of the present study. More precisely, Pearson correlations were run on the data, which are summarized in Table 6.4. These turned out to be strong and highly significant (at the 0.01 level). The level of significance was particularly remarkable between main clauses with tense auxiliaries and overall occurrence of transfer in main clauses ($r = 0.873**$, $p < 0.0001$). The same applied to the correlations between overall occurrence of transfer in main clauses and *total* occurrences when main and subordinate clauses were considered together ($r = 0.831**$, $p < 0.0001$). Indeed, the occurrence of interlanguage transfer with this type of auxiliary was a good indicator of transfer occurrence in the data ($r = 0.812**$, $p < 0.0001$). The scatterplot in Figure 6.1 illustrates these correlations.

Less strong correlations were found between main clauses with modal auxiliaries and overall occurrence of transfer ($r = 0.291**$, $p < 0.007$) or between main clauses with modal auxiliaries and total occurrences of

Table 6.3 Rate of occurrence of interlanguage transfer in L4 English: Raw scores and percentages

	Interlanguage transfer		No transfer	
	Tokens (Raw)	Tokens (Percentage)	Tokens (Raw)	Tokens (Percentage)
Discontinuous verb placement (*tense*)	93	94.9	5	5.1
Discontinuous verb placement (*modal*)	21	95.5	1	5
Discontinuous verb placement in main clause	114	95	6	5
Verb final in embedded clause	35	85.4	6	14.6
TOTAL CONTEXTS	149	92.6	12	7.4

Table 6.4 Internal consistency of interlanguage transfer

Interlanguage transfer of OV		Correlation coefficients
Discontinuous verb plac. (tense aux.)	Discontinuous verb placement	$r=0.873**$
	Total occurrences of transfer	$r=0.715**$
Discontinuous verb plac. (modal aux.)	Discontinuous verb placement	$r=0.291**$
	Total occurrences of transfer	$r=0.235*$
Discontinuous verb plac. (tense aux.)	Discontinuous verb plac. (modal aux.)	$r=0.980**$
Discontinuous verb plac.	Discontinuous verb plac.	$r=-0.369**$

interlanguage transfer ($r = 0.235*$, $p < 0.039$). However, given the relatively scarce creation of clauses with modal auxiliaries, it was difficult to observe how interlanguage transfer in these constructions related to other conditions. For example, only seven learners in the entire sample created contexts with both auxiliary types. What is important here is that whenever the two contexts were created, learners transferred in both of them. Hence, there was an almost perfect correlation between discontinuous verb placement with tense and modal auxiliaries in main clauses ($r = 0.980**$, $p < 0.0001$). Of particular interest were the results between transfer of discontinuous verb placement in main clauses and verb final

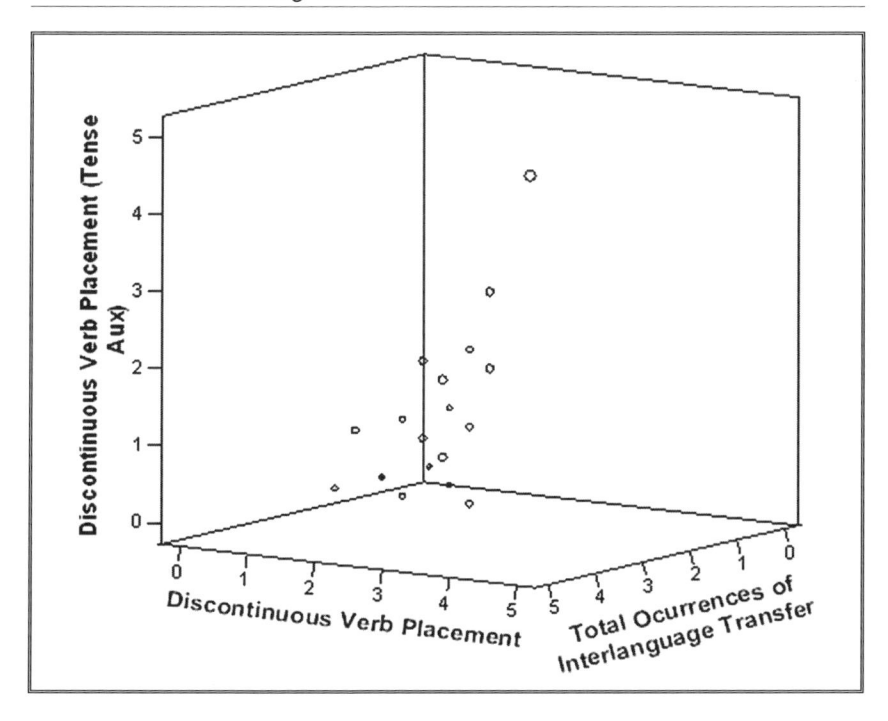

Figure 6.1 Scatterplot of interlanguage transfer

in subordinate clauses. In contrast to the coefficients reported so far, the type of correlation here was negative ($r = -0.369^{**}$, $p < 0.001$). This seems to indicate that development in main and subordinate clauses did not run parallel. This asynchronic development resulted in an inverse relationship between the two clause types. Hence, when learners were able to produce more sophisticated constructions including subordinate clauses, they had begun to progressively abandon the use of OV orders in main clauses, although these orders still persisted in embedded clauses.

Discussion and Conclusions

The present study contributes to the ongoing debate on the *psychotypological perspective* versus the *L2 factor perspective* in current research on Crosslinguistic Influence (CLI) in TLA. The qualitative and quantitative results reported here on the occurrence of interlanguage transfer from L3 German in L4 English seem to point out that typological closeness between the L1s Spanish and Catalan and the L4 English and typological distance between the L3 German and all the other languages in the area examined cannot discourage L3 activation and interlanguage transfer. To put it another way, at least within the context of limited exposure in the pre-pubertal learners examined here, in TLA, non-native languages may be activated more straightforwardly than the mother tongue, irrespective of typology. Hence, under the research conditions of this study, L2 status may be a better or more reliable predictor of interlanguage transfer. Yet, the effects of similarities between L3 German and L4 English cannot be underestimated for some similarities they present in the area of lexis. Specifically, the existence of neighbour words in the non-native languages affecting the lexical items that realise tense auxiliaries may also enhance the activation of L3 German (i.e. Ger. 'hat' and Eng. 'has'). However, the realization by the learners that these lexical items bear great resemblance in the L1s as well ('ha' in both Spanish and Catalan) would deem any of the background languages more or less equal candidates for transfer. Hence, the levels of activation of these items may differ from other lexical items in the exceptionally high level of activation they reach (see Sharwood Smith & Truscott, 2006: 210). In addition to this, similarities in lexis would contribute to explaining the high incidence in the present study of interlanguage transfer of discontinuous verb placement with tense auxiliaries but *not* with other linguistic properties (above all, VFINAL with simple verb phrases).

In view of the fact that the L3 investigated in this study is relatively distant from the L1s and the L4 in the area examined, one conclusion that can be drawn is that this typological distance might ultimately have an effect on the learners' representation of the linguistic system and, consequently, also on the activation of the L3 and the incidence of interlanguage transfer. In particular, if this was actually the case, German would be represented as relatively more separated from the other languages (i.e. Spanish, Catalan and English) because it is *relatively distant* in a given syntactic area and exhibits a different syntactic behaviour. However, further research on the linguistic constellation examined here should desirably address the role of typology in other linguistic levels (particularly in lexis) and check the results against those presented for the linguistic level investigated here. Indeed, this kind of investigation is already underway (Sanchez, forthcoming).

The reading of these findings as supportive of the *L2 factor perspective* is favoured also from a psycholinguistic point of view. Taking into consideration that the task employed was meant to keep the learner in a language-specific processing mode, one might expect the unintended language (i.e. L3 German) not to be activated during L4 production. Nonetheless, the data appear to prove that this is not the case. On the contrary, the levels of activation of the unintended language were very high (cf. Dewaele, 1998). The major implication of this, in De Groot *et al.* (2000: 426), is that these 'activation levels of the non-target language are completely beyond the participant's control'. If we take into consideration the potential (interlanguage) transfer at the lexicon–syntax interface indicated in the above paragraph, the learners' noticing of neighbour words might hinder the complete deactivation of L3 German during production in L4 English. More importantly, this would be a powerful argument in favour of language non-selectivity in TLA, that is, the route to the production of words in an L4 may be non-selective in multilinguals. The research agenda in TLA should include setting priorities based on CLI in relation to the lexicon–syntax interface, typology and language status in a more focused way, examining different language combinations in younger, older and adult learners in instructed and uninstructed acquisitional contexts. The pedagogical implications of such research would be of valuable help also for policy-makers, particularly as regards the age of the learner upon introduction of a second non-native language in the school curriculum.

Notes

1. Recently, this specific type of transfer has also been labelled *lateral transfer* (Jarvis & Pavlenko, 2008).
2. This investigation is supported by grant 135632-LLP-2007-UK-KA-1SCR from the European Commission and by project FFI2010-21478, funded by the Spanish Ministry of Education and Science. The author is grateful to these, and also to Grants 2002 FI00473 from the National Ministry of Education and 2005 BE 00687 from the Agency of University Financial Management and Research.
3. 'Grup de Recerca d'Adquisició de Llengües'.
4. The narratives in the BELC corpus have been coded according to the conventions of the CHAT sub-programme in CHILDES (Child Language System) and are available online at http://talkbank.org/data/SLA/.
5. The particle is a separable prefix to the verb.
6. In order to control for potential within-group age and instruction effects on these results and guarantee the comparability of the learners, a series of statistical tests were performed on the data. An analysis of variance was conducted with age as the independent factor. The result of this test was non-significant, $F(2,81) = 1.57$, $p = 0.951$. Post Hoc Scheffé comparisons: EG3 vs. EG4: $p = 0.986$; EG3 vs. EG5: $p = 0.975$; EG4 vs. EG5: $p = 0.961$. As for intensity of instruction in fifth graders, a t-test was run to compare the performance of groups EG5(A) and EG5(B). Again, this test did not find any significant difference ($p = 0.158$).

References

Abunuwara, E. (1992) The structure of the trilingual lexicon. *European Journal of Cognitive Psychology* 4, 311–322.
Afganova, L. (1997) Zur Frage des Lehrens und Lernens vom Deutschen als zweiter Fremdsprache nach dem Englischen in den neuen Schultypen in Russland (Oberstufe). *Zeitschrift für Interkulturellen Fremdsprachenunterricht* 2, 2–17.
Ahukana, J., Lund, N. and Gentile, J. (1981) Inter- and intra-lingual interference effects in learning a third language. *Modern Language Journal* 65, 281–287.

Bardel, C. and Lindqvist, C. (2007) The role proficiency and psychotypology in lexical cross-linguistic influence. A study of a multilingual learner of Italian L3. In M. Chini, P. Desideri, M.E. Favilla and G. Pallotti (eds) *Atti del VI Congresso di Studi dell'Associazione Italiana di Linguistica Applicata*, Napoi 9–10 February 2006 (pp. 123–145). Perugia: Guerra Editore.

Birdsong, D. (1992) Ultimate attainment in second language acquisition. *Language* 68, 706–755.

Bouvy, C. (2000) Towards the construction of a theory of cross-linguistic transfer. In J. Cenoz and U. Jessner (eds) *English in Europe. The Acquisition of a Third Language* (pp. 143–156). Clevedon: Multilingual Matters.

Cenoz, J. (2000) Research on multilingual acquisition. In J. Cenoz and U. Jessner (eds) *English in Europe. The Acquisition of a Third Language* (pp. 39–53). Clevedon: Multilingual Matters.

Cenoz, J. (2003) The role of typology in the organization of the multilingual lexicon. In J. Cenoz, B. Hufeisen and U. Jessner (eds) *The Multilingual Lexicon* (pp. 103–116). Dordrecht: Kluwer Academic.

Cenoz, J., Hufeisen, B. and Jessner, U. (eds) (2001a) *Cross-Linguistic Influence in Third Language Acquisition: Psycholinguistic Perspectives*. Clevedon: Multilingual Matters.

Cenoz, J., Hufeisen, B. and Jessner, U. (eds) (2001b) *Looking beyond Second Language Acquisition. Studies in Tri- and Multilingualism*. Tübingen: Stauffenburg Verlag.

Cenoz, J., Hufeisen, B. and Jessner, U. (eds) (2003) *The Multilingual Lexicon*. Dordrecht: Kluwer Academic.

Chandrasekhar, A. (1978) Base language. *International Review of Applied Linguistics* 16, 62–65.

Christen, H. and Näf, A. (2001) *Trausers, shoues* und *Eis* – Englisches im Deutsch von Französischsprachigen. In K. Adamzik and J. Christen (eds) *Sprachkontakt, -vergleich, -variation. Festchrist für Gottfried Kolde zum 65. Geburstag* (pp. 63–97). Tübingen: Max Niemeyer.

Chumbow, B. (1981) The mother tongue hypothesis in a multilingual setting. In *Proceedings of the Fifth Congress of the International Congress of l'Association Internationale de Linguistique Appliquée, Montréal August 1978* (pp. 42–55). Québec: Laval University Press.

Clyne, M. (1987) Constraints on code-switching – how universal are they? *Linguistics* 25, 739–764.

De Angelis (1999) Interlanguage transfer and Multiple Language Acquisition: a case study. Paper presented at TESOL 1999, New York City.

De Angelis, G. (2005) Multilingualism and non-native lexical transfer: An identification problem. *International Journal of Multilingualism* 2, 1–25.

De Angelis, G. (2007) *Third or Additional Language Acquisition*. Clevedon: Multilingual Matters.

De Angelis, G. and Selinker, L. (1999) Interlanguage transfer and multiple language acquisition: A case study. *Paper Presented at the Annual TESOL Conference, New York*.

De Angelis, G. and Selinker, L. (2001) Interlanguage transfer and competing linguistic systems in the multilingual mind. In J. Cenoz, B. Hufeisen and U. Jessner (eds) *Cross-linguistic Influence in Third Language Acquisition* (pp. 42–58). Clevedon: Multilingual Matters.

de Bot, K. (2004) The multilingual lexicon: Modelling selection and control. *International Journal of Multilingualism* 1, 17–32.

De Groot, A., Delmaar, P. and Lupker, S. (2000) Processing of interlexical homographs in translation recognition and lexical decision: Support for non-selective access to bilingual memory. *The Quarterly Journal of Experimental Psychology, Section A: Human Experimental Psychology* 53A, 397–428.

DeKeyser, R. (2000) The robustness of critical period effects in second language acquisition. *Studies in Second Language Acquisition* 22, 499–533.

DeKeyser, R. and Larson-Hall, J. (2005) What does the critical period really mean? In J. Kroll and A. De Groot (eds) *Handbook of Bilingualism: Psycholinguistic Approaches* (pp. 88–108). New York: Oxford University Press.

Dentler, S. (2000) Deutsch und Englisch – das gibt immer Krieg! In S. Dentler, B. Hufeisen and B. Lindemann (eds) *Tertiär-und Dritssprachen. Projekte und empirische Untersuchungen* (pp. 77–97). Tübingen: Stauffenburg Verlag.

Dewaele, J-M. (1998) Lexical inventions: French interlanguage as L2 versus L3. *Applied Linguistics* 19, 471–490.

Foote, R. (2009) Transfer in L3 acquisition: The role of typology. In Y-K. Leung (ed.) *Third Language Acquisition and Universal Grammar* (pp. 89–114). Bristol: Multilingual Matters.

Gawlitzek-Maiwald, I. (2000) 'I want a chimney builden': The acquisition of infinitival constructions in bilingual children. In S. Döpke (ed.) *Cross-linguistic Structures in Simultaneous Bilingualism* (pp. 123–148). Amsterdam: John Benjamins.

Hammarberg, B. (2001) Roles of L1 and L2 in L3 production and acquisition. In J. Cenoz *et al.* (eds) *Cross-linguistic Influence in Third Language Acquisition: Psycholinguistic Perspectives*. Clevedon: Multilingual Matters.

Hammarberg, B. (2009a) The languages of the multilingual: Some conceptual and terminological issues. *Paper Presented at the Sixth International Conference on Third Language Acquisition and Multilingualism*. Bolzano, Italy.

Hammarberg, B. (2009b) *Processes in Third Language Acquisition*. Edinburgh: Edinburgh University Press.

Heaton, B. (1966) *Composition through Pictures*. London: Longman.

Herdina, P. and Jessner, U. (2002) *A Dynamic Model of Multilingualism*. Clevedon: Multilingual Matters.

Huddleston, R. and Pullum, G. (2006) *A student's introduction to English Grammar*. Cambridge: Cambridge University Press.

Hufeisen, B. (1991) *Englisch als erste und Deutsch als zweite Fremdsprache. Empirische Untersuchungen zur fremdsprachlichen Interaktion*. Frankfurt: Peter Lang.

Hufeisen, B. (1993) Fehleranlyse: Englisch als L2 und Deutsch als L3. *International Review of Applied Linguistics* 31, 242–256.

Hufeisen, B. (2003) L1, L2, L3, L4, Lx – alle gleich? Linguistische, lernerinterne und lernerexterne Faktoren in Modellen zum multiplen Spracherwerb. In N. Baumgarten, C. Böttger, M. Motz and J. Probst (eds) *Übersetzen, Interkulturelle Kommunikation, Spracherwerb und Sprachvermittlung–das Leben mit mehreren Sprachen. Festschrift für Juliane House zum 60. Geburtstag. Didaktik und Methodik im Bereich Deutsch als Fremdsprache* (pp. 97–109).

Ilomaki, A. (2005) *Cross-linguistic Influence- A Cross-sectional Study with Particular Reference to Finnish-speaking and English-speaking Learners of German*. Unpublished ms.

Jaensch, C. (2009) L3 enhanced feature sensitivity as a result of higher proficiency in the L2. In Y-K. Leung (ed.) *Third Language Acquisition and Universal Grammar* (pp. 115–143). Bristol: Multilingual Matters.

Jarvis, S. and Pavlenko, A. (2008) *Crosslinguistic Influence in Language and Cognition*. New York: Routledge.

Jessner, U. (2008) A DST model of multilingualism and the role of metalinguistic awareness. *The Modern Language Journal* 92, 270–283.
Kellerman, E. (1983) Now you see it, now you don't. In S. Gass and L. Selinker (eds) *Language Transfer in Language Learning* (pp. 112–134). Rowley, MA: Newbury House.
Köberle, B. (1998) Positive Interaktion zwischen L2, L3, L4 und ihre Applikabilität im Fremdsprachenunterricht. In B. Hufeisen and B. Lindemann (eds) *Tertiärsprachen. Theorien, Modelle, Methoden* (pp. 89–109). Tübingen: Stauffenburg Verlag.
Larson-Hall, J. (2008) Weighing the benefits of studying a foreign language at a younger starting age in a minimal input situation. *Second Language Research* 24, 35–63.
Leung, Y-K. (2007) Third language acquisition: Why is it interesting to generative linguists? *Second Language Research* 23, 95–114.
Leung, Y-K. (2008) The verbal functional domain in L2A and L3A. Tense and agreement in Cantonese–English–French Interlanguage. In J. Liceras, H. Zobl and H. Gookluck (eds) *The Role of Formal Features in Second Language Acquisition.* (pp. 379–403). Mahwah: Erlbaum.
Lindemann, B. (2000) "Da fällt mir immer zuerst ein englischer Wort ein." Zum Einfluß der ersten Fremdsprache beim Übersetzen ins Deutsche. In S. Dentler, B. Hufeisen and B. Lindemann (eds) *Tertiär-und Dritssprachen. Projekte und empirische Untersuchungen* (pp. 57– 65). Tübingen: Stauffenburg Verlag.
Michiels, B. (1999) Die Rolle der Niederländischkenntnisse bei Französischsprachigen Lernern von Deutsch als L3: Eine empirische Intersuchung. *Zeitschrift für Interkulturellen Fremdsprachenunterricht* 3 (3), 1–43.
Möhle, D. (1989) Multilingual interaction in foreign language production. In H. Dechert and M. Raupach (eds) *Interlingual Processes* (pp. 179–194). Tübingen: Gunter Narr Verlag.
Müller-Lancé, J. (2003a) *Der Wortschatz romanischer Sprachen im Tertiärsprachererwerb*. Tübingen: Stauffenburg Verlag.
Müller-Lancé, J. (2003b) A strategy model of multilingual learning. In J. Cenoz, B. Hufeisen and U. Jessner (eds) *The Multilingual Lexicon* (pp. 117–132). Dordrecht: Kluwer Academic.
Muñoz, C. (ed.) (2006) *Age and the Rate of Foreign Language Learning*. Clevedon: Multilingual Matters.
Odlin, T. (1989) *Language Transfer*. Cambridge: Cambridge University Press.
Patkowski, M. (1980) The sensitive period for the acquisition of syntax in a second language. *Language Learning* 30, 449–472.
Ringbom, H. (1982) The influence of other languages on the vocabulary of foreign language learners. In G. Nickels and D. Nehls (eds) *Error Analysis, Contrastive Analysis, and Second Language Learning*. Heidelberg: IRAL.
Ringbom, H. (1987) Vocabulary: Influence from non-native languages. In H. Ringbom (ed.) *The Role of the First Language in Foreign Language Learning*. Clevedon: Multilingual Matters.
Ringbom, H. (2001) Lexical transfer in L3 production. In J. Cenoz, B. Hufeisen and U. Jessner (eds) *Cross-linguistic Influence in Third Language Acquisition: Psycholinguistic Perspectives* (pp. 59–68). Clevedon: Multilingual Matters.
Ringbom, H. (2007) *Cross-linguistic Similarity in Foreign Language Learning*. Clevedon: Multilingual Matters.
Ringbom, H. (2009) Paper presented at the Sixth International Conference on Third Language Acquisition and Multilingualism.

Sanchez, L. (forthcoming) Crosslinguistic influence in third language acquisition: English after German in bilingual Spanish/Catalan learners in an instructed setting.

Sanchez, L. and Jarvis, S. (2008) The use of picture stories in the investigation of crosslinguistic influence. *TESOL Quarterly* 42, 329–333.

Selinker, L. and Baumgartner-Cohen, B. (1995) Multiple language acquisition: "Damn it, why can't I keep these two languages apart?" *Language, Culture and Curriculum* 8, 115–121.

Shanon, B. (1991) Faulty language selection in polyglots. *Language and Cognitive Processes* 6, 339–350.

Sharwood Smith, M. and Truscott, J. (2006) Full transfer-full access: A processing-oriented interpretation. In S. Unsworth, T. Parodi, A. Sorace and M. Young-Scholten (eds) *Paths of Development in L1 and L2 Acquisition* (pp. 201–216). Amsterdam/Philadelphia: John Benjamins.

Sikogurika, M. (1993) Influence of languages other than the L1 on a foreign language: A case of transfer from L2 to L3. *Edinburgh Working Papers in Applied Linguistics* 4, 110–132.

Singh, R. and Carroll, S. (1979) L12, L2, and L3. *Indian Journal of Applied Linguistics* 4, 51–63.

Singleton, D. (1987) Mother- and other-tongue influence on learner French. *Studies in Second Language Acquisition* 9, 327–346.

Singleton, D. and Ó'Laoire, M. (2006) Psychotypology and the "L2 factor" in cross lexical interaction: An analysis of English and Irish influence in learner French. In M. Bendsten, M. Björklund, C. Fant and L. Forsman (eds) *Språk, lärande och ubtildning i sikte* (pp. 191–205). Vasa, Faculty of Edu: Åbo Akademi.

Stedje, A. (1977) Interferenz von Muttersprache und Zweitsprache auf eine dritte Sprache beim freien Sprechen- ein Vergleich. *Zielsprache Deutsch* 1, 15–21.

Tracy, R. and Gawlitzek-Maiwald, I. (2005) The strength of the weak: Asynchronies in the simultaneous acquisition of German and English. *Zeitschrift für Literaturwissenschaft und Linguistik* 35 (139), 28–53.

Tremblay, M-C. (2006) *Cross-Linguistic Influence in Third Language Acquisition: The Role of L2 Proficiency and L2 Exposure*. Cahiers Linguistiques d'Ottawa 34, 109–119.

Vogel, T. (1992) 'Englisch und Deutsch gibt es immer Krieg'. Sprachverarbeitungsprozese beim Erwerb des Deutschen als Drittsprache. *Zielsprache Deutsch* 23, 95–99.

Welge, P. (1987) Deutsch nach English. Deutsch als Dritte Sprache. In S. Ehlers and G. Kardener (eds) *Regionale Aspekte des Grundstudiums Germanistik* (pp. 189–225). München: Iudicum.

White, L. and Genesee, F. (1996) How native is near-native? The issue of ultimate attainment in adult second language acquisition. *Second Language Research* 12, 233–265.

Williams, S. and Hammarberg, B. (1993) *L1 and L2 Influence in L3 Production: Evidence from Language Switches*. Stockholm: Stockholm University.

Williams, S. and Hammarberg, B. (1998) Language switches in L3 production: Implications for a polyglot speaking model. *Applied Linguistics* 9, 295–333.

Wode, H., Rohde, A., Gassen F., Weiss, B., Jekat, M. and Jung, O. (1992) L1, L2, L3: Continuity vs. discontinuity in lexical acquisition. In P. Arnaud and H. Bejoint (eds) *Vocabulary and Applied Linguistics* (pp. 52–61). Hampshire: MacMillan.

Appendix

Chapter 7
Crosslinguistic Influence in Multilingual Language Acquisition: Phonology in Third or Additional Language Acquisition

EVA-MARIA WUNDER

Introduction

It was the linguist Scovel (1988) who identified the so-called 'Joseph Conrad phenomenon', which claims that it is impossible for an adult learner of a foreign language to achieve a native-like pronunciation. Scovel named it after the Polish-born British author Joseph Conrad, who acquired English only when he immigrated to England in 1878, aged 21, and managed to write some of the most famous novels in English with perfectly formed English syntax. His English pronunciation, however, retained a Polish accent throughout his life. For Scovel, this was proof of his hypothesis and reason enough 'to offer a free dinner to anyone who can show him an individual who learned a (sic!) L2 after puberty and who now speaks that L2 with perfect native pronunciation' (Tarone, 1987: 80). Apparently, the offer of April 1977 still stands.

The phenomenon of foreign accent in a non-native language is as old as foreign-language learning itself. A foreign accent is believed to come mostly from the learner's mother tongue (e.g. García Lecumberri & Gallardo, 2003; Pyun, 2005; Ringbom, 1987). However, a study by Hammarberg and Williams (1993) related another probable cause for foreign accent when learning a new non-native language, namely, influence from other non-native languages in the learner's mind.

A number of studies have already been conducted along the lines of this crosslinguistic influence (henceforth CLI) in multilingual acquisition (henceforth *L3/Ln acquisition*), the majority of them undertaken in the field of lexis (e.g. Cenoz, 2001; De Angelis & Selinker, 2001; Dentler, 2000; Dewaele, 1998; Ecke, 2001; Herwig, 2001; Möhle, 1989; Müller-Lancé, 2006; Vildomec, 1963). Moreover, an increasing number of studies on L3/Ln CLI in morphology and syntax have been carried out (e.g. Bardel, 2006; Bardel & Falk, 2007; Flynn *et al.*, 2004; Gibson *et al.*, 2001; Hammarberg, 2001; Klein, 1995). Likewise, CLI also seems to exist between a learner's non-native languages in the area of L3/Ln-phonology, for which only a small number of studies so far have attempted to find evidence (Gut, 2010; Hammarberg & Williams, 1993; Llama *et al.*, 2010; Pyun, 2005; Tremblay, submitted; Wrembel, 2010). To further investigate the validity of this fascinating hypothesis, the research question of this chapter will be as follows: Is there CLI on phonology between an adult multilingual speaker's non-native interlanguages?

Firstly, terminological clarifications will be the object of the next section, followed by a brief introduction to the concept of CLI and its conditioning factors in phonology. Subsequently, some recent studies on phonological CLI in L3/Ln are reviewed. The remaining sections relate the data and employed method for the present chapter, followed by the presentation and discussion of the findings in the ensuing sections.

Terminological Conundrums of Third or Additional Language Acquisition: Problematic Basic Concepts

Compared with second language learners (henceforth *L2 learners*), learners of a third or additional language (henceforth *L3/Ln learners*) have knowledge of at least two languages stored in their minds, have gained considerable metalinguistic awareness and are better equipped with learning strategies (e.g. Clyne *et al.*, 2004; Fouser, 2001; Ó Laoire, 2005). L3 and all subsequent foreign languages are grouped together in third or additional language acquisition, since the only difference manifests itself in the exponential increase in complexity of linguistic knowledge available in the learner's mind with each additional language. The acquisition processes, however, will proceed similarly, as far as is known to date, with the learner drawing on all their prior linguistic knowledge (e.g. Hall & Ecke, 2003; Ringbom, 2007). Multilingual learners subconsciously, or even consciously if more experienced, draw on this prior knowledge in all ensuing language learning. Because of the field's recent establishment, a few terminological challenges still remain, particularly with regard to naming a multilingual's languages.

Most scholars overgeneralise *L2* as an umbrella term for all non-native languages a speaker acquires, regardless, for example, of the chronology of acquisition. Instead, I will use *non-native languages* as a neutral cover term here. Moreover, the general terms *source language* (henceforth *SL*) and *target language* (henceforth *TL*) will be employed to illustrate the quality of the relationship between two or more languages involved in crosslinguistic transfer by a multilingual learner. A clear distinction will also be made in this chapter between the later acquired non-native languages, ranking them according to the order of acquisition: a multilingual speaker's native language is termed *L1*; the first non-native language to be acquired afterwards, *L2*; proceeding with *L3/Ln* as an umbrella term for any non-native language including and learnt beyond the chronologically third foreign language.

Crosslinguistic Influence: Types and Triggering Factors

The key concept of this chapter is that of CLI, a term coined by Sharwood Smith (1983) and Kellerman (1984). Interest in CLI has been strong in research throughout the last decades (e.g. Hammarberg & Williams, 1993; Ringbom, 1987, 2001; Schmidt & Frota, 1986; Selinker, 1992; Selinker & Baumgartner-Cohen, 1995; Sharwood Smith & Kellerman, 1986; Vildomec, 1963; Weinreich, 1953), and various definitions for the term *crosslinguistic influence* exist (e.g. Gass & Selinker, 1994; Kellerman, 1984; Odlin, 1989; Sharwood Smith, 1983). According to Odlin, a synonymous expression is that of *transfer* as a cover term for both negative interference and positive transfer from one or more languages to another. For this study, CLI is defined as the influence of prior linguistic knowledge on the production, comprehension and development of a TL (cf. De Angelis, 2007: 19), which can affect various linguistic levels, such as lexis, phonology, morphology or syntax. The most prominent influence can be seen in L3/Ln-lexis, mainly from the L1 but also from non-native languages, which several studies have been concerned with (e.g. Dentler, 2000; Ecke, 2001; Herwig, 2001; Müller-Lancé, 2006; Ringbom, 1987, 2001).

With multiple languages in a learner's mind, different types of CLI will appear. Traditionally, CLI occurs as a one-to-one type between a SL and a TL (cf. De Angelis, 2007: 20f). This is opposed to what has been termed *combined CLI* by De Angelis, 'the simultaneous influence of more than one language upon a target language, i.e. a many-to-one type' (2007: 21). However, in most cases, it will be rather difficult to attribute CLI to only one specific SL amongst several that may be interacting, which is the common type of CLI between multiple languages in an L3/Ln learner's mind. As in many areas of L3/Ln acquisition, research on combined CLI is rather scarce (e.g. Möhle, 1989; Singleton, 1987), probably because of the methodologically highly difficult task of differentiating the numerous potential SLs.

Moreover, types of CLI are distinguished according to the quality of transfer (i.e. into *negative* and *positive CLI*). The former refers to the transfer of different or similar but not identical items from the SL into the TL, leading to incorrect TL representations; the latter is the case when a particular item is found in the SL as well as the TL and can be transferred. Thus, acquisition is facilitated since it is easier for the learners to recognise or produce certain items in the TL, because they are already familiar with them from one or more SLs. As opposed to the learning of the L2, positive CLI in L3/Ln acquisition can also come from a feature that might exist in the non-native SL and TL, but not in the learner's L1. Unfortunately, this concept has not yet been sufficiently exploited in language teaching and learning, despite the doubtlessly facilitating effect it could have.

When acquiring a new language, different factors may contribute to CLI. A few studies have been conducted concerning significant variables (e.g. Cenoz, 2005; Dewaele, 1998; Ecke, 2001; Jessner, 2006; Odlin & Jarvis, 2004; Piske et al., 2001; Vogel, 1992). Depending on the linguistic level, certain factors might be significant and others not. For instance, the variables of age of learning (e.g. Cenoz, 2001), exposure to the non-native language (e.g. Fouser, 2001; Vildomec, 1963), order of acquisition (e.g. De Angelis, 2007), language distance (e.g. Clyne, 1997; De Angelis, 1999; De Angelis & Selinker, 2001; Rossi, 2006; Singleton, 1987), formal similarity (e.g. Rivers, 1979; Selinker & Baumgartner-Cohen, 1995) or perceived language distance (e.g. Möhle, 1989; Odlin, 1989; Ringbom, 1987; Singleton, 1987) have been shown to condition lexical CLI. Whether they also have an impact on L3/Ln-phonology remains to be investigated.

In studies on phonological CLI, though, to date, only *proficiency, recentness of use, foreign language effect* and *task relatedness* have been identified as factors contributing to CLI (e.g. Gut, 2010; Hammarberg & Hammarberg, 1993, 2005; Hammarberg & Williams, 1993; Llama et al., 2010; Pyun, 2005; Tremblay, submitted; Wrembel, 2010). With regard to proficiency, it is believed the more proficient that learners are in a non-native language other than the one they are acquiring at the moment, the more likely it is that CLI will occur from that SL in general (e.g. Hammarberg & Williams, 1998; Odlin & Jarvis, 2004; Ringbom, 1987; Schmidt & Frota, 1986; Singleton, 1987). With respect to proficiency in the TL, however, Hammarberg and Williams (1993, 1998) discovered that phonological CLI is most likely to occur in the initial stages of acquisition since the learner's command of the TL is still only very rudimentary and many knowledge gaps have to be filled with previously acquired linguistic information. CLI is also more likely to occur from languages the learners have made use of recently and, therefore, are still fresh in their minds and, consequently, accessed more easily, as a number of studies confirm (e.g. Dewaele, 1998; Flynn et al., 2004; Hammarberg & Williams, 1998; Vildomec, 1963). Regarding phonological CLI on a non-native TL, Hammarberg and Hammarberg (1993, 2005) as well as Hammarberg and Williams (1993) delivered corroborating evidence from their participant showing CLI from her L2, which was still very vivid to her because of her recent stay abroad. Meisel's (1983) concept of foreign language effect (also *L2 status*, Cenoz, 2001, or *foreign language mode*, De Angelis & Selinker, 2001; Selinker & Baumgartner-Cohen, 1995), referring to the fact that a certain language in question is categorised as a non-native language, also facilitates phonological CLI. Apparently, the similar acquisition processes and type of association established between two or more non-native languages in a learner's mind enables the learner to activate a prior non-native language more easily than the L1 when acquiring a new language (e.g. Gut, 2010; Llama *et al.*, 2010; Tremblay, submitted; Wrembel, 2010). Finally, Hammarberg and Williams (1993) showed in their study that phonological CLI could possibly be related to the type of task the L3/Ln learner has to perform: In a read-after-me task of an L3 text, the participant's pronunciation was coloured by the L1, whereas when faced with the more complex task of reading without a native speaker model, the L3 learner tended to rely on the L2 as a coping strategy.

A hierarchy seems to exist between these variables. Depending on the linguistic level, it is hypothesised that the various factors can accumulate until, for instance, a variable high up in the hierarchy comes into the equation and CLI is triggered. Only little research has been carried out so far on eliciting the real scope of potential influence of the single variables on the various linguistic levels, particularly with regard to eliciting significant factors for phonological CLI, or at least to corroborate previous findings.

Studies on Crosslinguistic Influence in L3/Ln-phonology

Although most studies concerning L3/Ln-phonology show that the L1 has the greatest influence (e.g. García Lecumberri & Gallardo, 2003; Hammarberg & Hammarberg, 1993; Llisterri & Poch, 1987; Ringbom, 1987; Pyun, 2005), the groundbreaking and most important longitudinal study to date delivered astonishing results. Hammarberg and Williams (1993) investigated CLI in the L3/Ln-phonology of an L1 English speaker with native-like proficiency in her L2 German and no previous knowledge in the TL Swedish. Recordings were made during Sarah's acquisition process of her L3 Swedish oral productions in natural conversation with a Swedish native speaker followed by a picture-story narration in the form of either a dialogue or a monologue, as well as read-on-your-own and read-after-me tasks in the early stages. The impact of Sarah's high proficiency in her L2 German, which additionally was still fresh in her mind from a long stay in Germany, and her strong wish to avoid sounding English in the L3 Swedish, manifested itself in CLI from the L2 German in her L3 productions in the initial stages. However, as Sarah's L3 skills were honed and automaticity in L3 production increased, the L2 CLI gradually weakened. This reliance on another non-native language seemed to be a strategy in order to cope with new, unfamiliar L3 phonetic forms, whereas later on, when Sarah had abandoned this insufficient strategy and focused more on direct

L3 production, only CLI from the L1 persistently prevailed as a basic constraint. Thus, reliance on the L2 in the initial stages of L3 acquisition appeared to be due to the fact that she wanted to avoid CLI from the L1 as well as that she had easy access to her L2, and that it was situation-dependent on the demand of a speech task. This above-mentioned task-related variation seemed to condition the use of the L2 articulatory settings in her L3.

Wrembel (2010) reported similar findings in her study investigating the degree of CLI from the L1 and L2, using foreign accent ratings by expert judges. Her 60 L1 Polish participants with very good L2 German and different proficiencies in the TL English were recorded reading out a text as well as speaking freely, and the samples were then rated for overall degree of foreign accent. Wrembel discovered CLI from the L1 and the L2, with the relative strength differing depending on the proficiency level in the TL, just as Hammarberg and Hammarberg (1993, 2005) or Hammarberg and Williams (1993, 1998) concluded.

One of the scarce studies conducted in the area of phonological CLI that cannot clearly confirm the hypothesis of the L2 having influence on the L3/Ln, however, is that of Gut (2010). To examine the features of vowel reduction and speech rhythm, she recorded her participants reading out a text and retelling it, as well as producing free speech in both their L2 and L3. Her first analysis, looking into whether CLI from the L1 in the L2 or L3 phonological system can be observed, produced negative findings. Moreover, judging from the participants' heterogeneous values for vowel reduction and speech rhythm in both the L2 and L3, no positive CLI from the L2 could be indicated at all. However, despite non-existent vowel reduction in their L1 and the existent one in their L2, the participants produced some reduction in L3, which could alternatively be interpreted as positive L2 CLI.

Voice Onset Time in German, British English and Castilian Spanish

Every language possesses a specific articulatory basis with unique features, such as final devoicing in German or nasalised vowels in Portuguese. To be able to tell whether CLI from the L2 of the participants has occurred or not, a unique articulatory feature that then might appear in the TL has to be looked at more closely. Therefore, the feature of aspiration in the stressed syllable-initial voiceless stops /p t k/ was chosen for the present chapter to investigate potential CLI. Assessing the amount of aspiration is operationalised by measuring along the continuum of *voice onset time* (henceforth *VOT*). VOT is defined as 'the interval (measured in milliseconds) between the release of the articulators (the opening of the lips, the dropping of the tongue, etc.) and the beginning of regular vocal chord pulses' (Nathan et al., 1987: 205). If the pulses substantially precede the release of the articulators, the sound is voiced and VOT is negative; if the pulses start simultaneously or only a very short time after, the sound is voiceless and unaspirated, with VOT around 0 ms; if the pulses start some time after, though, the segment is voiceless and aspirated and VOT is positive, which is the phenomenon to be examined in this study.

VOT was chosen because the presence or absence of the correct amount of aspiration is one of the reasons for speech to be perceived as accented (cf. Nathan et al., 1987: 204). Moreover, VOT is a feature that allows the establishment of a straightforward relationship between the languages investigated in this chapter, namely, German as L1, British English as L2, and Castilian Spanish as TL. In all three phonological systems exists the dichotomy of a group of the voiced stops /b d g/ and the voiceless stops /p t k/. However, they are produced differently in each language. Aspiration in German and English is an allophonic feature. For instance, in English, the voiceless stops in stressed syllable-initial position followed by a syllable-nuclear voiced segment are aspirated, as is going to be examined, such as in *part, tone* or *cold* (cf. Laver, 1995: 351), except for when the stops are preceded by /s/ or appear in a word-internal stressed onset position (cf. Llama et al., 2010). Moreover, voiceless stops in stressed onset positions followed by a voiced syllable-marginal resonant (i.e. /r/, /l/, /j/ or /w/) are also aspirated (cf. Laver, 1995: 351), for example in *cry, plane, cure* or *tweed*.

For the participants' L1 German, following previous research (Angelowa & Pompino-Marschall, 1985; Jessen, 1998; Mansell, 1979) and the analysis of the speech of three L1 German speakers recorded as a control group, average values of between 30 ms and 45 ms for /p/, 40 ms and 55 ms for /t/, and between 45 ms and 60 ms for /k/ were assumed for this study. For British English, again in accordance with the literature (Azou et al., 2000; Lisker & Abramson, 1964; Llama et al., 2010) and a control recording, average VOT values for English were set between 60 ms and 100 ms, with VOT for /p/ ranging between 60 ms and 70 ms; for /t/, between 70 ms and 80 ms; and for /k/, between 80 ms and 100 ms. In Spanish, however, there is no aspiration. For the present study, after consultation of previously established values (Llama et al., 2010; Rosner et al., 2000) and a control recording, it was decided on Spanish VOT values of between 0 ms and 15 ms for /p/, between 15 ms and 20 ms for /t/, and between 20 ms and 30 ms for /k/. Thus, to sum up, there is only minor aspiration in the stressed onset position for voiceless stops in German, a great deal of aspiration in English, and almost none in Spanish. Consequently, to find much aspiration in the participants' Spanish would translate to CLI from their L2 English. To produce the correct amount of aspiration in a non-native language generally seems to be quite difficult to achieve for a foreign language learner. Most of the time, stops are realised with VOT values in between native speaker values with *hybrid* or *compromise VOT* (e.g. Flege, 1995; Moyer, 2004).

Studies Investigating Crosslinguistic Influence on the Acquisition of Aspiration Patterns in L3/Ln Acquisition

To be able to pin down phonological CLI on the basis of a concrete feature, Tremblay (submitted) and Llama *et al.* (2010) decided to investigate VOT and the acquisition of aspiration patterns for the voiceless stop consonants /p t k/. Tremblay (submitted) measured the VOTs of her four L1 English participants with L2 French who were beginners of L3 Japanese to elicit which language exerts influence on L3 VOT values when VOT is produced differently in all prior languages. The participants were asked to read out a word list as well as perform a delayed repetition task to investigate a potential task effect. However, contrary to Hammarberg and Williams' (1993) findings, Tremblay found no statistically significant task-relatedness. With regard to differentiating between their L1 English and L2 French aspiration, though, the analysis yielded longer VOT values in the L1. Interestingly, VOT in the L2 and L3 were found to be quite similar, in fact almost native-like in the TL. Therefore, the approximated L3 values to L2, not L1, exhibit an influence of L2 on L3, as was also the result of Hammarberg and Williams.

The second study after Tremblay, seeking further support for Hammarberg and Williams, also operationalised on the basis of measurement of aspiration, was conducted by Llama *et al.* (2010). They compared VOT measurements of TL Spanish word list recordings of one group of nine participants with L1 English and L2 French with those of a second group consisting of nine L1 speakers of French with L2 English. To ensure that L1, L2 and L3 had an equal chance to become the SL for CLI, preliminary small talk was conducted in the L1, then the L2 word list reading followed, and finally, the L3 word list reading as well as a picture description in Spanish was performed. The analysed data was then coded for aspiration or no aspiration. A high percentage of aspirated tokens would signify English influence, whereas a low percentage would point to French influence. Although mean percentage of aspiration of the L1 English group was higher, though not statistically significant, Llama *et al.* still observed quite balanced CLI in the L3 from English as well as French as a SL across both groups of participants. Moreover, measuring the respective L2 values from the word lists, the researchers found that both groups showed hybrid L2 VOTs. When comparing the latter with the L3 values, they discovered that in accordance with their very high similarity, the L2 VOT values seemed to have been transferred into the learners' L3. Regardless, Llama *et al.* also take into consideration, after looking at the mean VOT values of all participants, that the L1 had possibly already influenced the L2 whilst acquiring it, which resulted in hybrid L2 VOT. Thus, the similar L2–L3 VOT values could have an underlying L1 effect through prior influence on the learners' L2. As discussed before, this phenomenon is what De Angelis (2007) calls *combined CLI*. There is, thus, inconclusive evidence for the role of CLI from a non-native language in phonological acquisition. The study described in the following empirical part of this chapter aims to shed more light on this question.

Data and Method

Participants

Eight participants consented to being recorded and to fill in a questionnaire: five of them female, and three male. For comparative reasons, all of them spoke German as L1 and English as L2, except for participant 4, who lived in Romania as a child and learnt Romanian as L2, followed by English as L3 at the age of 12. Moreover, all participants were learners of the TL Spanish, perceiving their proficiency as that of beginners to advanced beginners, except for participants 2 and 5 who considered themselves advanced learners of Spanish. Apart from participants 3 and 8, all participants had knowledge of at least one non-native language besides English and Spanish. In addition to the eight participants, one native speaker of British English and Castilian Spanish, as well as three L1 speakers of German were recorded and their speech analysed to arrive at additional reference VOT values to the mean VOT values reported in the literature for native speakers of German, English and Spanish.

At the time of recording, five participants were taking the Spanish beginners' course *Lengua española 2* at the Language Centre at the University of Augsburg taught by native speakers of Spanish. Participant 2 had attended it previously, whereas participants 1 and 3 had, so far, only completed *Lengua española 1*, the four-month introductory course, which is similarly structured to *Lengua española 2*. The first intensive course of six hours per week, equalling approximately 90 hours per term, suffices to achieve a beginners' level of Spanish.

Data

Each participant was recorded performing two read-on-your-own tasks. For that, they were instructed to read out a text at their own pace, firstly in their L2 English (or L3, in the case of participant 4 – PART4) and then in the TL Spanish. As mentioned above, this task is supposed to elicit non-L1 influence, since the learners have to rely more on their prior linguistic knowledge than on only trying to imitate like in a read-after-me task with a native speaker model, which, in turn, is assumed to elicit L1 CLI. Consequently, they were expected to show influence from their strongest non-native language, which from self-evaluation, except for PART4 and PART5, was English.

For the recordings, an English nonsense text (cf. Appendix) of approximately one minute was devised specifically to elicit numerous realisations of /p t k/ in potentially aspirated position, as well as a Spanish text (cf. Appendix) of similar length, which had been modified to raise the number of /p t k/ tokens. To avoid any bias, the participants were only told beforehand that the recordings would be used to investigate overall CLI, and were informed afterwards that this would be done by analysing the degree of aspiration in their productions of /p t k/.

Like all participants, the native speaker models of German, British English and Castilian Spanish were each recorded reading out the respective text in their L1. The German text (cf. Appendix) of similar length was also devised as a nonsense text to elicit as many tokens of /p t k/ in aspirated position as possible. All in all, the recordings of the eight participants yielded 113 tokens of /p/, 135 of /t/ and 73 of /k/ in aspirated position in English, and 67 tokens of /p/, 40 of /t/ and 107 of /k/ in non-aspirated position in Spanish. The recordings were made using a 24-bit Edirol audio recorder. Mono wave format was chosen at a sampling rate of 44 kHz for reasons of accurate time-segmentation alignment.

Data Analysis

To avoid intuitive and sometimes impressionistic judgement of native speaker listeners, the recordings were analysed for VOT, which was defined earlier as the interval in milliseconds between the release of the articulators and the beginning of regular vocal chord pulses, with the speech analysis software Praat (Boersma & Weenink, 2007; version 4.6.32). Firstly, in each recording, the utterances containing /p t k/ in stressed syllable-initial, potentially aspirated position were transcribed orthographically on one tier. Afterwards, the voiceless stops were isolated on a second tier by setting a boundary in the waveform at the point of the burst of air (i.e. the release of the articulators) indicated by the highest amplitude in the waveform. The values were also included for weak releases with small amplitudes if a clear burst was still visible. Moreover, where double or multiple bursts occurred, VOT was measured with the first burst as the starting point of aspiration. A second boundary was set exactly at the point of zero-crossing on the vertical axis of the first regular vocal chord pulse (i.e. the first regular wave of the following

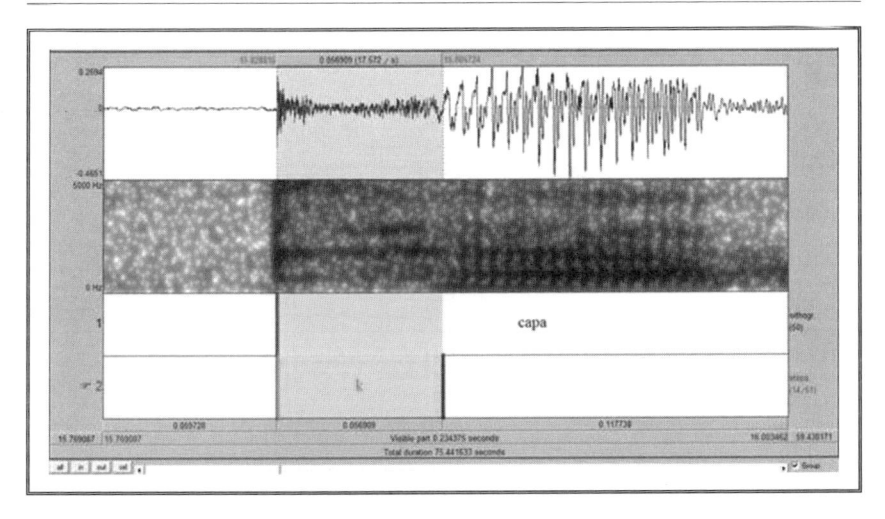

Figure 7.1 Example of an annotation with Praat of a Spanish reading passage

sound). The interval between these two boundaries constitutes VOT or aspiration, as can be seen in Figure 7.1.

Mean learner VOT values were then compared with the values of the native speaker model recordings, as well as with L1 VOTs for German, English and Spanish established in previous studies. Finally, to explore a potential relationship between L2 and L3/Ln, the data were submitted to statistical analyses, namely, the calculation of the correlation between English and Spanish mean values for /p t k/. Ambiguous tokens and individual mispronunciations resulting in stress shifts, affrication or doubtful beginnings of periodic waves were not included.

Discussion of Results

Measurements conducted to evoke CLI on the production of voiceless stops /p t k/ in stressed onset position in the participants' L2 English and L3/Ln Spanish yielded the mean VOT values presented in Table 7.1.

With regard to potential SLs for CLI on the TL phonological system, Figure 7.2 shows their distribution for all non-native-like VOTs of L3/Ln Spanish /p t k/. Similar to Llama *et al.*'s (2010) findings, my participants also seem to exhibit mainly an L1 effect on the TL, with 31.8% of the non-native VOT values for Spanish /p t k/ situated within the L1 German range. None clearly demonstrate CLI only from the L2, contradicting findings of previous research (e.g. Hammarberg & Williams, 1993; Llama *et al.*, 2010). Influence of the L2 on the TL Spanish occurs together only with the L1 as the aforementioned combined CLI in 18.2% of the cases. Moreover, hybrid values constitute the largest group (50%), that is,

Table 7.1 Mean VOT values (in ms) for each participant's productions of voiceless stops in stressed onset position in L2 English and L3/Ln Spanish

	VOT /p/ (in ms)		VOT /t/ (in ms)		VOT /k/ (in ms)	
	L2 E	L3/Ln S	L2 E	L3/Ln S	L2 E	L3/Ln S
PART1	62	48	75	37	90	52
PART2	78	26	98	24	112	42
PART3	47	34	73	46	74	59
PART4	60	17	72	19	75	35
PART5	38	20	51	23	71	34
PART6	62	54	73	60	85	66
PART7	50	33	73	46	83	59
PART8	30	12	64	29	86	35

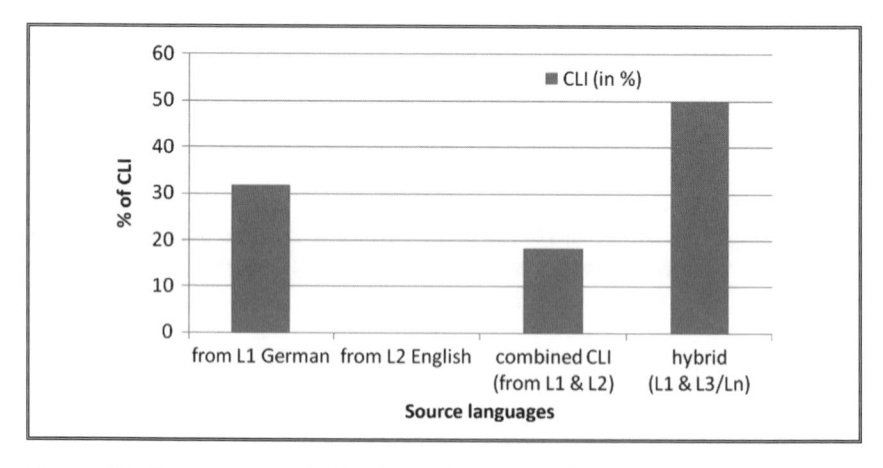

Figure 7.2 Percentages of CLI from the source languages onto all participants' non-native-like L3/Ln Spanish productions of /p t k/ and hybrid VOTs

instances in which it cannot be determined whether VOTs were influenced by L1 German or native-like Spanish.

To arrive at the mentioned SL distribution, the VOTs measured in the read-on-your-own task and displayed in Table 7.1 were compared with the previously established values for native-like aspiration and assigned to a certain L1 range, or in between, strictly according to the cut-off values (cf. Table 7.2). As can be seen from PART1's values, her English

Crosslinguistic Influence in Multilingual Language Acquisition   117

Table 7.2 Assignment of VOTs of non-native-like productions of /p t k/ to L1 German range (/p/ 30–45 ms, /t/ 40–55 ms, /k/ 45–60 ms), L1 English range (/p/ 60–70 ms, /t/ 70–80 ms, /k/ 80–100 ms), L1 Spanish range (/p/ 0–15 ms, /t/ 15–20 ms, /k/ 20–30 ms) or hybrid values

	VOT /p/ (in ms)		VOT /t/ (in ms)		VOT /k/ (in ms)	
	L2 English	L3/Ln Spanish	L2 English	L3/Ln Spanish	L2 English	L3/Ln Spanish
PART1	62	48	75	37	90	52
	native-like	p$_S$ (→G/E)	native-like	t$_S$ (→S/G)	native-like	k$_S$ (→G)
PART2	78	26	98	24	112	42
	native-like	p$_S$ (→S/G)	native-like	t$_S$ (→S/G)	native-like	k$_S$ (→S/G)
PART3	47	34	73	46	74	59
	p$_E$ (→G/E)	p$_S$ (→G)	native-like	t$_S$ (→G)	native-like	k$_S$ (→G)
PART4	60	17	72	19	75	35
	native-like	p$_S$ (→S/G)	native-like	native-like	k$_E$ (→G/E)	k$_S$ (→S/G)
PART5	38	20	51	23	71	34
	p$_E$ (→G)	p$_S$ (→S/G)	t$_E$ (→G)	t$_S$ (→S/G)	k$_E$ (→G/E)	k$_S$ (→S/G)
PART6	62	54	73	60	85	66
	native-like	p$_S$ (→G/E)	native-like	t$_S$ (→G/E)	native-like	k$_S$ (→G/E)
PART7	50	33	73	46	83	59
	p$_E$ (→G/E)	p$_S$ (→G)	native-like	t$_S$ (→G)	native-like	k$_S$ (→G)
PART8	30	12	64	29	86	35
	p$_E$ (→G)	native-like	t$_E$ (→G/E)	t$_S$ (→S/G)	native-like	k$_S$ (→S/G)

productions of /p t k/ are within the interval of L1 values, contrary to the mixed results for Spanish. Her L3/Ln VOTs all deviate from those expected from native speakers: /k/ clearly falls into the range of L1 German means, whereas /p/ lies in between German and English values, and /t/ lies between Spanish and German ones. PART2 also exhibits native-like VOTs for her L2 English stops, yet none of her L3/Ln Spanish productions can be attributed clearly to either her L1 or her L3/Ln. Results obtained for PART3's productions of English /t/ are located within L1 range, but the VOTs for /p/ and /k/ are situated in between German and English values. However, examining his L3/Ln tokens yields mean VOT values adequate for L1 German /p t k/. PART4 is the only participant to render native-like values for /t/ in both her L2 English and her L3/Ln Spanish, as well as for her English productions of /p/. Yet, her means for Spanish /p/ and /k/ lie between Spanish and German, whereas her English VOTs for /k/ reflect values in between German and English. Rather mixed results were yielded from the measurements of PART5's stop productions. All her VOTs deviate from L1 values. Her English /p/ and /t/ means are distinctly German, and her English /k/ is situated in between German and English VOTs. Moreover, none of her Spanish tokens can be clearly assigned to either Spanish or German values. PART5 tends to produce very weak stop releases, which sometimes result in almost voiced tokens, for instance in *planes*, *cuanto*, *tras* or *cúal*. The latter are not included in her mean VOTs. Like PART5's L3/Ln stops, PART6 produces all Spanish /p t k/ non-native-like. Interesting to note, however, is that her Spanish VOT means are located in between German and English values, a unique phenomenon in all tokens examined. Unfortunately, PART6 also shows many stress shifts, which reduces her number of analysable tokens. Regarding her English stops, they all reflect L1 means. PART7's average productions of English /t/ and /k/ can also be clearly assigned to L1 values. Nevertheless, his English /p/ lies between German and English native values. On the other hand, all his L3/Ln Spanish stops are situated in the L1 German interval. PART8 curiously presents native-like values in his L3/Ln Spanish productions of /p/, but L1 German ones for his mean L2 VOTs of /p/. Further, he presents native-like English /k/, yet the Spanish counterpart exhibits intermediate values between Spanish and German. Regarding the production of /t/, he shows non-native-like VOT in both L2 and L3/Ln, with the English means falling between German and English values, and Spanish means ranging between Spanish and German.

All in all, the analysis yields rather heterogeneous results regarding CLI. However, most results also corroborate findings on the influence of place of articulation on VOT values; that is, the longest values are generally found for /k/ and the shortest for /p/ in both English and

Spanish. The most conspicuous result, though, seems to be a quite evident L1 effect on both English and Spanish productions, which confirms previous findings by García Lecumberri and Gallardo (2003), Hammarberg and Hammarberg (1993), Llisterri and Poch (1987), Ringbom (1987) and Pyun (2005). For instance, PART5 shows mean VOTs situated between German and Spanish for her L3/Ln stops. Interesting to note is that her L2 tokens already exhibit German influence, which seems to have been transferred further onto the L3/Ln. This underlying L1 effect is also visible in the L3/Ln Spanish VOT means of /p/ and /k/ of PART3 or of PART7's /p/. The reason might be, to a certain degree, inherent to the feature of VOT itself. Previous research in the field of second language acquisition established that acquiring VOTs comparable to native-speaker values in the L2 is achieved only rarely (e.g. Caramazza et al., 1973; Díaz-Campos, 2004; Fellbaum, 1996). Instead, the L2 learners rather tend to retain some L1 features in their L2, thus creating hybrid VOTs (e.g. Flege & Eefting, 1987; Laufer, 1996). This can be seen, for example, in the mean values of PART5, where L1 influence leads to the creation of intermediate VOTs in her productions of English /k/, which exhibit means between L1 German and L1 English cut-off values.

Generally speaking, there are four conceivable constellations for the analysis of the stop productions, namely, native-like VOTs in both L2 English and L3/Ln Spanish; native-like English but non-native-like Spanish productions; non-native English and native-like Spanish mean VOTs; and finally, non-native values for both L2 and L3/Ln. However, with regard to CLI from non-native languages investigated in this chapter, the second constellation is of the main interest. According to the previously discussed variables, CLI from English should only occur from native-like L2 productions onto the L3/Ln, which subsequently displays non-native-like VOTs, either distinctly influenced by one specific language or situated in between two languages, showing hybrid values.

Depending on whether mean VOTs in Spanish were located within the range of the L1 cut-off values established above or in between mean VOTs of L1 Spanish, German or English, it translated to distinct influence from either one or two languages. Generally speaking, intermediate mean L3/Ln VOTs within L1 German range would be interpreted as German influence, whereas relatively high VOTs located in the L1 English interval would be attributed to L2 influence. As can be inferred from Table 7.1, the analysis yields rather mixed results. For instance, in PART1's speech, L1 influence on the production of L3/Ln Spanish /k/ was measured, but values obtained for Spanish /p/ could not be assigned clearly to either German or English, and L3/Ln /t/ ranged in between Spanish and German.

A few learners, such as PART4 or PART8, seem to have been able to establish phonetic categories in the sense of Flege's (1995) *Speech Learning Model* for L2 English and L3/Ln Spanish productions of /p t k/ similar to those of L1 speakers. PART4, for example, shows native-like VOT values for /t/ in both her L2 and L3/Ln as well as in L2 tokens of /p/. This might either indicate advanced proficiency in her L3/Ln Spanish, or she simply acquired native-like VOT. It could also be connected to a higher meta-linguistic awareness because PART4 had already attained native speaker proficiency in her L2 Romanian at a very early age and, consequently, might approach acquisition of further non-native phonological systems more efficiently than less experienced language learners (e.g. Ó Laoire, 2005; Thomas, 1988). Since Romanian, like Spanish, also exhibits no aspiration of stops in stressed onset positions, a fourth possibility would be L2 CLI onto PART 4's TL Spanish.

In the case of PART5, whose L2 mean VOT for /k/ is already influenced by the L1 German, thus creating a hybrid L2 value, it is conceivable that it could have been transferred further into the L3/Ln TL Spanish. The third language would have been added to the feature concoction and would have created another compromise value between Spanish and German. This would signify that, to some degree, CLI from the L2 has occurred, with the compromise L2 value instigating the creation of a hybrid TL form. In reality, looking at PART5's mean VOTs for /k/ across both L2 and L3/Ln, they show a difference of 37 ms. However, in the case of PART3's values for /p/, they only differ by 13 ms, with the similar mean values pointing to transferred hybrid VOT. Secondly, some of these compromise VOTs could also indicate combined influence from the L1 and L2 on L3/Ln productions (cf. De Angelis, 2007). PART1 and PART6 are the only participants to display values that cannot be clearly attributed to one SL. Although PART1 displays a VOT mean of 48 ms for her L3/Ln /p/, VOTs for all of PART6's L3/Ln stops are located in between cut-off values for L1 German and L1 English, with 54 ms for /p/, 60 ms for /t/, and 66 ms for /k/, with both participants thus indicating the aforementioned combined CLI.

Expressed in percentages, all participants produced 62.5% of L2 English stops with native-like VOT values, more specifically 50% of /p/, 75% of /t/ and 62.5% of /k/, illustrating the required advanced proficiency for the L2 to potentially become a SL for phonological CLI. In comparison, only 8.3% of all tokens of L3/Ln Spanish stops are produced with the correct amount of aspiration in the TL, that is, 12.5% of /p/ and /t/ and 0% of /k/ (cf. Figure 7.3). Bearing in mind that we are dealing with beginners of Spanish, the percentage producing already native-like VOTs points to the conclusion that either the proficiency level of these participants is higher than that of beginners and their L3/Ln phonological system is already beyond the stage for CLI to occur from

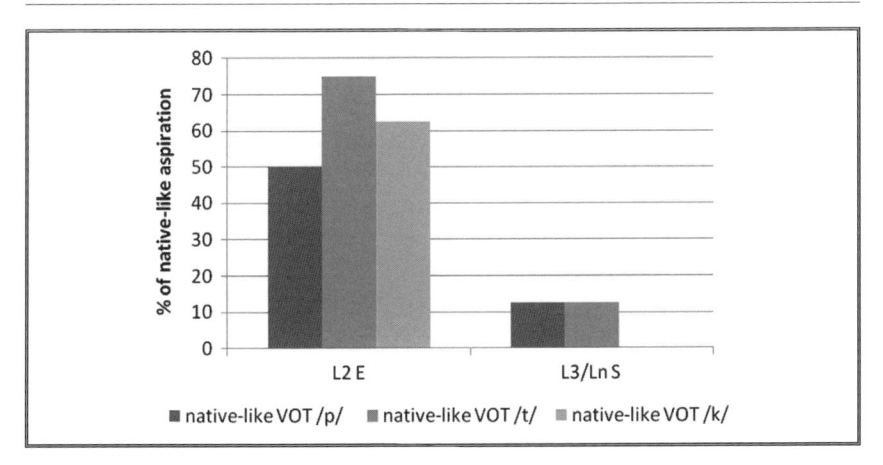

Crosslinguistic Influence in Multilingual Language Acquisition   121

Figure 7.3 Amount of native-like VOTs (in%) of all participants in L2 English and L3/Ln Spanish productions of /p t k/

non-native languages or we might be dealing with individual cases of native-like acquisition of VOT, as previously mentioned.

Concerning any influence coming from the L2 English, as already mentioned, it was only visible in combined CLI. However, it is also conceivable that there might have been L2 influence on the L3/Ln productions located within German L1 values, as will be argued in the following paragraphs. Firstly, looking at several L2 tokens (PART3's /p k/, PART4's /k/, PART5's /k/, PART7's /p/ and PART8's /t/), they are all produced with compromise VOT situated in between German and English L1 means. Analogous to the aforementioned L1 influence transferred from these L2 hybrid values onto the L3/Ln, resulting in mean VOTs located in between L1 Spanish and German, it is probable that existing influence from the L2 features of the compromise values was also transferred. This transfer of L2 features would result in higher mean L3/Ln values compared with those influenced by only the L1. Thus, it could be hypothesised that these L3/Ln VOTs situated within L1 German range and, therefore, showing higher VOTs than Spanish–German intermediate ones might either be due solely to L1 influence or maybe to hybrid L2 influence, which could have had some effect in that it has raised the Spanish aspiration rate, though only up to L1 German level.

Looking at the means, PART3 seems to be the only participant to possibly have also incorporated L2 influence in his L3/Ln productions of /k/, which display VOT means of 74 ms in the L2 and 59 ms in the L3/Ln. All others with L2 hybrid values either show Spanish–German L3/Ln compromise values or already present L2 hybrid VOTs situated closer to L1 German than English. Yet, this is only a hypothesis, and with the present data or existing methodologies it is impossible to determine exactly where the influence came from or whether it occurred at all. Perhaps the hybrid values displayed by the participants simply reflect chance results or idiosyncratic pronunciations.

To explore the relationship between the L2 English as a potential SL for phonological CLI and the TL Spanish, the $v = 24$ pairs of VOT (L2 English; L3/Ln Spanish) measurements listed in Table 7.1 were considered as a sample for which the correlation coefficient r was calculated. With the resulting value $r = 0.44$ and $v - 2 = 22$ degrees of freedom, the significance level of r was determined at $p = 0.05$ using a table of two-sided confidence limits of Student's t-distribution. That means, at an admissible error probability of 5%, the existence of a certain, though not very strong relationship between L2 English and L3/Ln Spanish can be assumed. Applying this procedure to the mean VOT values for /p t k/ separately did not yield statistically significant results either.

Conclusions

The present study was conducted to elicit the CLI of non-native languages in the phonology of eight L3/Ln learners of Spanish with L1 German and L2 English. This was operationalised by measuring aspiration, that is, VOT of voiceless stops in stressed onset position. The values obtained for all participants were then compared to native-speaker VOTs. Results turned out to be rather mixed, and most tokens displayed means located in between two languages. As can be seen in Table 7.1, some CLI from the L2 existed, but a prominent L1 influence was also detected. Moreover, a number of tokens were already realised native-like.

Taking everything into consideration, it has to be acknowledged that this chapter contradicts rather than corroborates previous findings of non-native languages exerting phonological CLI on an L3/Ln TL (e.g. Hammarberg & Williams, 1993; Llama *et al.*, 2010; Pyun, 2005; Tremblay, submitted). It was not possible to produce clear evidence for L2 English influence on the acquisition of L3/Ln Spanish aspiration patterns. This may not least also be due to certain limitations of this study.

Firstly, because only eight learners consented to being recorded, the number of analysed tokens was quite limited. In future research, the number of participants should be increased, and a different instrument than a read-on-your-own text task, such as word lists, could be used to elicit more qualitatively high tokens. A larger group would also allow for more control of the variability across task results. Moreover, despite efforts to record a homogeneous population, the participants of this study possibly deviated from this ideal. For instance, some participants might have already been beyond the stage for phonological CLI to occur from a non-native language; they might have been too proficient in the TL, as they exhibited considerable L1 influence, which is supposedly characteristic for the advanced stages of the acquisition of a new phonological system (Hammarberg & Williams, 1993).

Although the correct perception of sounds, which according to Flege (1995) seems to be the basic premise for preventing foreign accent, cannot be taught (yet) unfortunately, it is feasible to raise metalinguistic awareness for the 'hot spots' in a TL phonological system, that is, for very similar but not identical sounds. Thus, learners may be directed to more awareness of the probability of CLI, be it negative or potential positive transfer. Incorporating the prior linguistic knowledge of learners and trying to channel it in the classroom by showing up what can and what cannot be transferred could also help facilitate the acquisition of a new phonological system. There is still a lot of work to be done. However, if effective learning strategies and teaching methods can be developed and successfully implemented, Mr Scovel will, in due course, have to host a dinner banquet.

Acknowledgement

Many thanks to Anton Wunder for his help with the statistical analyses.

References

Angelowa, T. and Pompino-Marschall, B. (1985) Zur akustischen Struktur initialer Plosiv-Vokal-Silben im Deutschen und Bulgarischen. *Forschungsberichte des Instituts für Phonetik und sprachliche Kommunikation der Universität München* 21, 83–96.

Azou, P., Ozsancak, C., Morris, R.J., Jan, M., Eustache, F. and Hannequin, D. (2000) Voice onset time in aphasia, apraxia of speech and dysarthria: A review. *Clinical Linguistics and Phonetics* 14, 131–150.

Bardel, C. (2006) La connaissance d'une langue étrangère romane favorise-t-elle l'acquisition d'une autre langue romane? Influences translinguistiques dans la syntaxe d'une L3. *Acquisition et Interaction en Langue Étrangère* 24, 149–180.

Bardel, C. and Falk, Y. (2007) The role of the second language in third language acquisition: The case of Germanic syntax. *Second Language Research* 23 (4), 459–484.

Boersma, P. and Weenink, D. (2007) Praat. Doing phonetics by computer (Version 4.6.32). On WWW at http://www.praat.org. Accessed 23.10.07.

Caramazza, A., Yeni-Komshian, G., Zurif, E. and Carbone, E. (1973) The acquisition of a new phonological contrast: The case of stop consonants in French–English bilinguals. *The Journal of the Acoustical Society of America* 54, 421–428.

Cenoz, J. (2001) The effect of linguistic distance, L2 status and age on cross-linguistic influence in third language acquisition. In J. Cenoz, B. Hufeisen and U. Jessner (eds) *Cross-linguistic Influence in Third Language Acquisition: Psycholinguistic Perspectives* (pp. 8–20). Clevedon: Multilingual Matters.

Cenoz, J. (2005) Learning a third language: Cross-linguistic influence and its relationship to typology and age. In B. Hufeisen and R. Fouser (eds) *Introductory Readings in L3* (pp. 1–9). Tübingen: Stauffenburg Verlag.

Clyne, M. (1997) Some of the things trilinguals do. *The International Journal of Bilingualism* 1 (2), 95–116.

Clyne, M., Hunt, C. and Isaakidis, T. (2004) Learning a community language as a third language. *International Journal of Multilingualism* 1 (1), 33–52.

De Angelis, G. (1999) Interlanguage transfer and multiple language acquisition: A case study. *Paper Presented at TESOL, New York City,* 1999.

De Angelis, G. (2007) *Third or Additional Language Acquisition.* Clevedon: Multilingual Matters.

De Angelis, G. and Selinker, L. (2001) Interlanguage transfer and competing linguistic systems in the multilingual mind. In J. Cenoz, B. Hufeisen and U. Jessner (eds) *Cross-linguistic Influence in Third Language Acquisition: Psycholinguistic Perspectives* (pp. 42–58). Clevedon: Multilingual Matters.

Dentler, S. (2000) Deutsch und Englisch – das gibt immer Krieg! In S. Dentler, B. Hufeisen and B. Lindemann (eds) *Tertiär- und Drittsprachen. Projekte und empirische Untersuchungen* (pp. 77–97). Tübingen: Stauffenburg Verlag.

Dewaele, J-M. (1998) Lexical inventions: French interlanguage as L2 versus L3. *Applied Linguistics* 19 (4), 471–490.

Díaz-Campos, M. (2004) Context of learning in the acquisition of Spanish second language phonology. *Studies in Second Language Acquisition* 26, 249–273.

Ecke, P. (2001) Lexical retrieval in a third language: Evidence from errors and tip-of-the-tongue states. In J. Cenoz, B. Hufeisen and U. Jessner (eds) *Cross-linguistic Influence in Third Language Acquisition: Psycholinguistic Perspectives* (pp. 90–114). Clevedon: Multilingual Matters.

Fellbaum, M.L. (1996) The acquisition of voiceless stops in the interlanguage of second language learners of English and Spanish. On WWW at http://www.asel.udel.edu/icslp/cdrom/vol3/663/a663.pdf. Accessed 6.12.08.

Flege, J. (1995) Second language speech learning: Theory, findings, and problems. In W. Strange (ed.) *Speech Perception and Linguistic Experience: Issues in Cross-Linguistic Research* (pp. 233–277). Baltimore: York Press.

Flege, J. and Eefting, W. (1987) Production and perception of English stops by native Spanish speakers. *Journal of Phonetics* 15, 67–83.

Flynn, S., Foley, C. and Vinnitskaya, I. (2004) The cumulative-enhancement model of language acquisition: Comparing adults' and children's patterns of development in first, second and third language acquisition of relative clauses. *International Journal of Multilingualism* 1 (1), 3–16.

Fouser, R. (2001) Too close for comfort? Sociolinguistic transfer from Japanese into Korean as an L ≥ 3. In J. Cenoz, B. Hufeisen and U. Jessner (eds) *Cross-linguistic Influence in Third Language Acquisition: Psycholinguistic Perspectives* (pp. 149–169). Clevedon: Multilingual Matters.

García Lecumberri, M. and Gallardo, F. (2003) English EFL sounds in school learners of different ages. In M. del Pilar García Mayo and M. García Lecumberri (eds) *Age and the Acquisition of English as a Foreign Language* (pp. 115–135). Clevedon: Multilingual Matters.

Gass, S. and Selinker, L. (eds) (1994) *Language Transfer in Language Learning.* Amsterdam: John Benjamins.

Gibson, M., Hufeisen, B. and Libben, G. (2001) Learners of German as an L3 and their production of German prepositional verbs. In J. Cenoz, B. Hufeisen and U. Jessner (eds) *Cross-linguistic Influence in Third Language Acquisition: Psycholinguistic Perspectives* (pp. 138–148). Clevedon: Multilingual Matters.

Gut, U. (2010) Cross-linguistic influence in L3 phonological acquisition. *International Journal of Multilingualism* 7 (1), 19–38.

Hall, C.J. and Ecke, P. (2003) Parasitism as a default mechanism in L3 vocabulary acquisition. In J. Cenoz, B. Hufeisen and U. Jessner (eds) *The Multilingual Lexicon* (pp. 71–85). Dordrecht: Kluwer Academic.

Hammarberg, B. (2001) Roles of L1 and L2 in L3 production and acquisition. In J. Cenoz, B. Hufeisen and U. Jessner (eds) *Cross-linguistic Influence in Third Language Acquisition: Psycholinguistic Perspectives* (pp. 21–41). Clevedon: Multilingual Matters.

Hammarberg, B. and Hammarberg, B. (1993) Articulatory re-setting in the acquisition of new languages. *Phonum* 2, 61–67.

Hammarberg, B. and Hammarberg, B. (2005) Re-setting the basis of articulation in the acquisition of new languages: A third-language case study. In B. Hufeisen and R. Fouser (eds) *Introductory Readings in L3* (pp. 11–18). Tübingen: Stauffenburg Verlag.

Hammarberg, B. and Williams, S. (1993) A study of third language acquisition. In B. Hammarberg (ed.) *Problem, Process, Product in Language Learning* (pp. 60–69). Stockholm: Stockholm University Press.

Hammarberg, B. and Williams, S. (1998) Language switches in L3 production: Implications for a polyglot speaking model. *Applied Linguistics* 19 (3), 295–333.

Herwig, A. (2001) Plurilingual lexical organization: Evidence from lexical processing in L1–L2–L3–L4 translation. In J. Cenoz, B. Hufeisen and U. Jessner (eds) *Cross-linguistic Influence in Third Language Acquisition: Psycholinguistic Perspectives* (pp. 115–137). Clevedon: Multilingual Matters.

Jessen, M. (1998) *Phonetics and Phonology of Tense and Lax Obstruents in German*. Amsterdam: John Benjamins.

Jessner, U. (2006) *Linguistic Awareness in Multilinguals: English as a Third Language*. Edinburgh: Edinburgh University Press.

Kellerman, E. (1984) The empirical evidence for the influence of the L1 in interlanguage. In A. Davies, C. Criper and A. Howatt (eds) *Interlanguage* (pp. 98–122). Edinburgh: Edinburgh University Press.

Klein, E. (1995) Second versus third language acquisition: Is there a difference? *Language Learning* 45 (3), 419–465.

Laufer, C. (1996) The acquisition of a complex phonological contrast: Voice timing patterns of English initial stops by native French speakers. *Phonetica* 53, 86–110.

Laver, J. (1995) *Principles of Phonetics*. Cambridge: Cambridge University Press.

Lisker, L. and Abramson, A. (1964) A cross-language study of voicing in initial stops: Acoustical measurements. *Word* 20, 384–422.

Llama, R., Cardoso, W. and Collins, L. (2010) The roles of typology and L2 status in the acquisition of L3 phonology: The influence of previously learnt languages on L3 speech production. *International Journal of Multilingualism* 7 (1), 39–57.

Llisterri, J. and Poch, D. (1987) Phonetic interference in bilingual's learning of a third language. *In Proceedings XIth ICPhS. The Eleventh International Congress of Phonetic Sciences* (Vol. 5, pp. 134–137). Tallinn, Estonia: Academy of Sciences of the Estonian SSR. On WWW at http://liceu.uab.es/ ~ joaquim/publicacions/ Llisterri_Poch_87_L3_Bilinguals.pdf. Accessed 16.12.08.

Mansell, P. (1979) The articulation of German plosives. *Forschungsberichte des Instituts für Phonetik und sprachliche Kommunikation der Universität München* 11, 1–207.

Meisel, J. (1983) Transfer as a second language strategy. *Language and Communication* 3, 11–46.

Möhle, D. (1989) Multilingual interaction in foreign language production. In H. Dechert and M. Raupach (eds) *Interlingual Processes* (pp. 179–194). Tübingen: Narr.

Moyer, A. (2004) *Age, Accent, and Experience in Second Language Acquisition: An Integrated Approach to Critical Period Inquiry.* Clevedon, Avon, UK: Multilingual Matters.

Müller-Lancé, J. (2006) *Der Wortschatz romanischer Sprachen im Tertiärspracherwerb: Lernstrategien am Beispiel des Spanischen, Italienischen und Katalanischen.* Tübingen: Stauffenburg Verlag.

Nathan, G., Anderson, W. and Budsayamongkon, B. (1987) On the acquisition of aspiration. In G. Ioup and S. Weinberger (eds) *Interlanguage Phonology: The Acquisition of a Second Language Sound System* (pp. 204–228). Cambridge, MA: Newbury House Publishers.

Odlin, T. (1989) *Language Transfer. Cross-linguistic Influence in Language Learning.* Cambridge: Cambridge University Press.

Odlin, T. and Jarvis, S. (2004) Same source, different outcomes: A study of Swedish influence on the acquisition of English in Finland. *International Journal of Multilingualism* 1 (2), 123–140.

Ó Laoire, M. (2005) L3 in Ireland: A preliminary study of learners' metalinguistic awareness. In B. Hufeisen and R. Fouser (eds) *Introductory Readings in L3* (pp. 47–55). Tübingen: Stauffenburg Verlag.

Piske, T., Flege, E. and MacKay, I. (2001) Factors affecting degree of foreign accent in an L2: A review. *Journal of Phonetics* 29, 191–215.

Pyun, K. (2005) A model of interlanguage analysis: The case of Swedish by Korean speakers. In B. Hufeisen and R. Fouser (eds) *Introductory Readings in L3* (pp. 55–70). Tübingen: Stauffenburg Verlag.

Ringbom, H. (1987) *The Role of the Mother Tongue in Foreign Language Learning.* Clevedon: Multilingual Matters.

Ringbom, H. (2001) Lexical transfer in L3 production. In J. Cenoz, B. Hufeisen and U. Jessner (eds) *Cross-linguistic Influence in Third Language Acquisition: Psycholinguistic Perspectives* (pp. 59–68). Clevedon: Multilingual Matters.

Ringbom, H. (2007) *Cross-linguistic Similarity in Foreign Language Learning.* Clevedon: Multilingual Matters.

Rivers, W. (1979) Learning a sixth language: An adult learner's daily diary. *The Canadian Modern Language Review* 36 (1), 67–82.

Rosner, B., López-Bascuas, L., García-Albea, J. and Fahey, R. (2000) Voice-onset times for Castilian Spanish initial stops. *Journal of Phonetics* 28, 217–224.

Rossi, S. (2006) L'interférence lexical dans l'acquisition d'une troisième langue: Effet langue seconde ou distance typologique? Unpublished master's thesis, University of Calgary, AB, Canada. On WWW at http://acpi.scedu.umontreal.ca/fr/acpi_depot/consulter.php?PHPSESSID = 111e9e15c0e3c7ed6dbb7fcb22cd48c8. Accessed 17.12.08).

Schmidt, R. and Frota, S. (1986) Developing basic conversation ability in a second language: A case study of an adult learner of Portuguese. In R. Day (ed.) *Talking to Learn: Conversation in Second Language Acquisition* (pp. 237–326). Rowley, MA: Newbury House.

Scovel, T. (1988) *A Time to Speak: A Psycholinguistic Inquiry into the Critical Period for Human Speech.* Cambridge, MA: Newbury House.

Selinker, L. (1992) *Rediscovering Interlanguage.* London: Longman.

Selinker, L. and Baumgartner-Cohen, B. (1995) Multiple language acquisition: 'Damn it, why can't I keep these two languages apart?' *Language, Culture and Curriculum* 8 (2), 115–121.

Sharwood Smith, M. (1983) On first language loss in the second language acquirer: Problems of transfer. In S. Gass and L. Selinker (eds) *Language Transfer in Language Learning* (pp. 222–231). Rowley, MA: Newbury House.
Sharwood Smith, M. and Kellerman, E. (1986) *Crosslinguistic Influence in Second Language Acquisition*. New York: Pergamon Press.
Singleton, D. (1987) Mother and other tongue influence on learner French: A case study. *Studies in Second Language Acquisition* 9, 327–346.
Tarone, E. (1987) The phonology of interlanguage. In G. Ioup and S. Weinberger (eds) *Interlanguage Phonology: The Acquisition of a Second Language Sound System* (pp. 70–85). Cambridge, MA: Newbury House Publishers.
Thomas, J. (1988) The role played by metalinguistic awareness in second and third language learning. *Journal of Multilingual and Multicultural Development* 9 (3), 235–246.
Tremblay, M-C. (submitted) Voice onset time in the L3 Japanese of L1 English-L2 French bilinguals. *International Journal of Multilingualism*.
Vildomec, V. (1963) *Multilingualism*. Netherlands: A.W. Sythoff-Leyden.
Vogel, T. (1992) 'Englisch und Deutsch gibt es immer Krieg': Sprachverarbeitungsprozesse beim Erwerb des Deutschen als Drittsprache. *Zielsprache Deutsch* 23 (2), 95–99.
Weinreich, U. (1953) *Languages in Contact*. New York: Linguistic Circle.
Wrembel, M. (2010) L2-accented speech in L3 production. *International Journal of Multilingualism* 7 (1), 75–90.

Appendix

L1 German stimulus text

Papa Peter tut nicht viel. Meistens parkt er seinen Porsche auf Theas Platz oder kauft überflüssige Putzmittel ein. Peter kann einen wirklich zum Toben bringen. Thea und ihre Tochter Cara finden das auch und trompeten Peter öfter den Marsch. Dann parkt Peter ausnahmsweise mal nicht seinen Porsche auf Theas Platz und kauft nur ein Putzmittel. Aber kaum ist ein Tag vergangen, hat Peter Thea und Cara total vergessen. Typisch Papa Peter.

L2 English stimulus text

Paul, a pretty cute and clever boy of 20 years, previously used to be a tedious pupil. In his spare time, Paul loved collecting toy planes, as well as playing and listening to tunes, for example, by *The Cure, Toto* or *Creed*. One day, he came across a really cute girl named Chloe and was hit by Cupid's arrow straight away. It triggered the most extraordinary feelings within him. His tummy seemed to continually twitch with excitement, and Paul felt a tiny bit queasy. At a party, he finally took enough courage to talk to Chloe, mainly about his tunes and planes. It turned out that Chloe and Paul were totally incompatible: she was terrified of planes and listened to Paris Hilton's terrible music. That was the end of Paul and Chloe.

L3/Ln Spanish stimulus text

El viento norte y el sol porfiaban todo el tiempo sobre cuál de ellos era el más fuerte, cuando acertó a pasar un príncipe envuelto en ancha capa. Convinieron en que quien antes lograra obligar al príncipe a quitarse la capa sería considerado más poderoso. El viento norte sopló con gran furia todo el día, pero cuanto más soplaba, más se arrebujaba en su capa el príncipe. Por fin, tras tanto esfuerzo, el viento norte abandonó la empresa. Entonces brilló el sol con ardor, e inmediatamente se despojó de su capa el príncipe, por lo que el viento norte hubo de reconocer la superioridad del sol.